The Narrow Path

To: Pastor Frank L. Thomas Sr.
may this book be a
blessing to you!

Elijah Hayes

Elijah Hayes
(AKA John)

ISBN 978-1-64492-600-0 (paperback)
ISBN 978-1-64492-601-7 (digital)

Christian Faith Publishing, Inc.
832 Park Avenue
Meadville, PA 16335
www.christianfaithpublishing.com

Printed in the United States of America

Enter ye in at the strait gate; for wide is the gate and broad is the way that leadeth to destruction, and many there be which go in thereat.

—Matthew 7:13

Because strait is the gate, and narrow is the way which leadeth unto life, and few there be that find it.

—Matthew 7:14

Contents

Introduction

This is a book of prayer and devotions to open the eyes of Christians that have fallen into sin and makes no excuses for sin. This book has been inspired by the Holy Spirit; God the Father; and Jesus Christ, the Son of God. If anyone has an ear, let them hear, thus says the Spirit of God.

I have always been a seeker of the Truth. I believe there is only one way to gain access to heaven; and therefore, there is only one truth and that is my Lord and Savior, Jesus Christ.

And I say to all the people of the world, please try Jesus. You will not regret it. If you humble yourselves and ask Jesus into your heart, you can be transformed by His words, as are in the King James Bible. As you read the Bible, the words will come alive and jump off the page and into your heart and you will find a peace in your spirit that you never knew before. That is the Holy Spirit confirming with your spirit that what you are reading is the Truth.

To the Christians that are living in sin, the Spirit of the Lord says, "Wake up!" We are living in the last days before Jesus returns. There is a war in the spiritual realm that is raging. Satan never sleeps, and he has legions of demons that want to destroy Christianity. They will attack the church from without and from within. The attacks from without come from other religions and from the secular world. The attacks from within the Christian church are more subtle. These attacks can range from the corruption of the message from the preachers and teachers to the personal destruction of the individual member of the body of Christ. I have experienced many attacks from both within and without. It is my prayer that every Christian will have victory in this war. Amen.

This is not a war of guns and bombs. It is a war of internal corruption and spiritual decay. It is time for all Christians to put on the full armor of God. The Christian church has been preaching a sermon that has been watered down with secular humanism. The Church is like a lion that has had its claws and teeth removed. How can we be victorious over sin in our lives when some Christian churches put sinners in the pulpits to spew out doctrines of devils? It is time for a spiritual cleansing that has to start with the individual Christian. One by one we are to open our eyes and ears and turn from our wicked ways. I say "we" because I admitted my guilt before my Lord and have sought him day and night until I received my healing from my sins. And I will say this, it was not until I did this that I felt a closeness to Jesus that I never knew before. I could go on about my life, but that is not the purpose of this book. I pray this book helps to put people on the narrow path that Jesus spoke of! Amen.

Part One

The Plans of God

"Because straight is the gate, and narrow is the way, which leadeth unto life, and few there be that find it" (Matt. 7:14).

There is a narrow path that we must stay on. This is the path that Jesus talked about in Matthew 7:14. He said that only a few will find this path and stay on it.

I have found this narrow path, and I want to help others to find it also. The narrow path is a course in life that is a merging of the spiritual with the physical. It is destiny to be realized as we walk down a road that leads us into a future of spiritual meaning and purpose. With the help of the Holy Spirit, I will try to explain the best I can what God has shown me. There are several steps one must take to first get near the narrow path before one can think about walking down that path. I will list these steps as prerequisites to finding the path, then I will describe the path.

Step 1 - You must accept Jesus Christ as your Lord and Savior, acknowledging that you are a sinner and repenting. You are asking Jesus to come into your heart and live in you. Jesus said in the book of John 3:3, "Verily, verily, I say unto thee, except a man be born again, he cannot see the kingdom of God."

Step 2 - Make a public confession of your faith by being baptized by immersion. Jesus said in Matthew 10:32, 33, "Whosoever therefore shall confess me before men, him will I confess also before my Father which is in heaven. But whosoever shall deny me before men, him will I also deny before my Father which is in heaven."

Step 3 - Find a good Bible-believing church and attend regularly. Get involved with your church, fellowship with other like-minded Christians, and help spread the good news of the gospel to a lost world by supporting the missionaries financially and with your prayers.

These three steps are necessary as your foundation in Christ. Now on this foundation you will build a life of service to God, family, and country. It is important to have enough faith to be able to say that you believe in Jesus Christ as the only way to God and heaven. There can be no room for doubting this. If you believe there are many ways and religions that all lead to God, then you will never find the narrow path. So set your mind on Christ and Christ alone. For all glory belongs to Jesus and He will share none of it with any false Gods, religions, or beliefs.

> "Enter ye in at the straight gate: for wide is the gate
> and broad is the way that leadeth to destruction, and
> many there be which go in thereat" (Matt. 7:13).

Survival

Now after completing steps 1, 2, and 3, you are a born-again Christian. You have been adopted into the body of Christ, and your name has been written into the Book of Life. Is all okay and well with your soul? No, not really. There are some things you now need to know in order to survive as a Christian. I will list them below:

1. Satan wants to destroy you. You are in a battle of good vs. evil. Before you were born again, Satan was not too focused

on you because you were already his. Now that you are born again, prepare for war. Your soul is at stake.

2. You can lose your salvation if you fall for Satan's lies. His biggest lie is you can never lose your salvation. This has given many Christians a false sense of security, to go so far as to openly live in sin without a repentant heart to change. This kind of teaching makes the Crucifixion of Christ a mockery. Shame on you, false preachers. Wake up! If a Christian could not lose salvation, then why would the devil waste his time and energy to tempt the born-again Christian to sin? There is too much emphasis put on the fact that our salvation is a free gift. Jesus is not Santa Clause. He does not come around at Christmas to hand out free gifts to sinners. Jesus made a way for us to be saved, but it came at a terrible price. Jesus Christ was crucified on a cross. The most horrible way to die. His blood paid the price for our salvation. There is always a price to be paid for salvation. And millions of Christians have paid the price by being put to death for their faith in Christ. The freedom that we enjoy in America are not free but were paid for by the men and women that fought for our country. Some paid the price with their lives, and many became disabled for life. The sad thing is this, if they could see the moral decay and the lack of respect for our flag today, they would say, "Is this what we fought for?"

"Be not deceived; God is not mocked: for whatsoever a man soweth, that shall he also reap" (Gal. 6:7)

"And the Jew's Passover was at hand, and Jesus went up to Jerusalem, and found in the temple those that sold oxen and sheep and doves, and the changers of money sitting: And when he had made a scourge of small cords, he drove them all out of the temple, and the sheep, and the oxen; and poured out the changers' money, and overthrew the tables; And said unto them that sold doves, 'Take these things hence; make not my Father's house an house of merchandise.' And his disciples remembered that it was written, The zeal of thine house hath eaten me up" (John 2:13–17).

3. There is a lifestyle that has to be different from the worldly majority. There is a way to live that is a living sacrifice to God. Jesus calls us to a high standard of living that surpasses that of the scribes and Pharisees of his day. We are not to look at statues of the Catholic saints and adore them and say they were holy. As born-again Christians, we are all called to be saints and to live a holy life. Will we ever be perfect and free from sin? No, never! Only Jesus was perfect and never sinned. When we fall from grace we become stained and dirty, but the precious blood of Jesus is able to cleanse us and restore us. We need to be aware of what is *sin*. The Word of God will convict us if we believe what is written in the Bible. We are not to judge others, we need to judge ourselves and let God judge the world.

The Kingdom

"For I say unto you, that except your righteousness exceed the righteousness of the scribes and Pharisees, ye shall in no case enter into the kingdom of heaven" (Matt. 5:20).

4. There is a supernatural power in prayer and fasting. A Christian that doesn't pray is like a hunter without a weapon. Pray every day. Take time to talk to God.
5. There are angels that help us. Don't worship them; they are there to help us battle against demonic forces.

"I fell down to worship before the feet of the angel which shewed me these things. Then said he unto me, see thou do it not: for I am thy fellow servant, and of thy brethren the prophets, and of them which keep the sayings of this book: worship God" (Rev. 22:8–9).

6. The Bible is God's way to communicate to man. It is a vast warehouse of wisdom and knowledge and power. We need to study God's word every day. If you do, you will be blessed.

   Turn away from all manner of sin. Do not run with the old crowd; separate yourselves from the drunkards and fornicators. You have been called to a life of holiness. Stop destroying yourself with alcohol, tobacco, and drugs. Your body is a temple of the Holy Spirit; treat it with respect. Don't act holy on Sunday and live like the devil the rest of the week.

7. Commit to holiness. Make your home a safe and secure refuge for your family.

8. Love your spouse, in sickness and in health, for better or worse.

9. Be patient with your family and friends; love them and they will love you. Go out of your way to help one another. Forgive them when they need forgiveness. Love is what Jesus taught us.

10. Critique your motives, judge yourself, and search yourself for sin and faults. Purify yourself so you can help others.

11. Be kind and gentle; be committed to God. Help your family, friends, and neighbors.

    Reach out to the stranger; feed the hungry; clothe the naked; give water to the thirsty; help the elderly, the weak and disabled, the widows and orphans, the starving and homeless; be kind to the animals; be a good steward to our planet; support those wanting to end pollution; do not exploit the downtrodden; pay the worker a fair wage; don't be greedy for gain; be satisfied with having the basics; give thanks; say grace before eating; be neat, organized, and orderly.

12. Support your church, not the TV preachers that use your money to live a lavish lifestyle.

13. Repent when you mess up and sin, then ask for the power to be free from that sin. Jesus came to offer forgiveness for our sins and to deliver us from being a slave to sin. Deliverance is a ministry that can set the captive free from the demons that are out to destroy us. When the disciples tried to cast out the demon, they couldn't. When they asked Jesus why, he rebuked them for not having enough faith.

Deliverance

"And he said unto them, 'This kind can come forth by nothing, but by prayer and fasting'" (Mark 9:29).

Jesus was referring to demons.

"But the very hairs of your head are all numbered" (Matt. 10:30 and 39).

We serve a mighty God! Not only does God know how many hairs on our head, but he knows our every thought, the thoughts of every person on earth, every second of the day, every day, at the same time. How awesome is that?

Thank you, Jesus, for that narrow path. I feel safe here. No evil can touch me. When my mind is on you, Lord, I feel protected by your holy presence. You put your angels in charge of helping me. You called me out of the darkness and put me into your wonderful light.

Satan, I rebuke you in the name of Jesus Christ.

Satan, I resist your temptations in the name of Jesus Christ.

I will not stray off course. My feet are planted on solid rock. I will not be moved.

I rebuke the wind, in the name of Jesus Christ; I will not be blown off the path that is set before me.

When I reach the end of the path, I will commit my spirit to God. Jesus, lead me home to that mansion in heaven that you have prepared for me!

The Big Lie

> "Wherefore God also gave them up to unclean-
> ness through the lusts of their own hearts, to
> dishonor their own bodies between themselves.
> Who changed the truth of God into a lie, and
> worshipped and served the creature more than
> the Creator, who is blessed forever. Amen."
> (Rom. 1:24, 25).

In many churches today, you have the blind leading the blind. When was the last time you heard a preacher call out to repent or face the hell fire that awaits the person living in sin? I am a firm believer in a church having an altar call after the sermon. Not just for healing or financial blessings, but for repenting of sins. But the most important call is accepting Jesus and coming forward as a public demonstration of that first step of faith in Christ.

People want to hear an easy, feel-good message. They want to be reassured of going to heaven. They want to be healed of sickness and receive blessings of prosperity. The "prosperity preachers" are making millions by preaching a false gospel, and the "easy-way-to-heaven preachers" are also filling their pockets with your hard-earned cash. They want you to believe that just because you said the sinner's prayer, that you have a ticket to heaven. Why, they will tell you to close your eyes and repeat this prayer silently if you don't want anyone to see you. That's okay, we won't even ask you to get out of your seat. We won't even ask you to repent. Why not? Because they are afraid of the devil? Or are they afraid to offend someone? Was Jesus afraid to offend? Not at all. As a matter of fact, the apostle Paul says in the book of Romans 9:33, "As it is written, Behold, I lay in Sion a stumbling-stone and rock of offence: and whosoever believeth on him shall not be ashamed."

> "It is easier for a camel to go through the eye of
> a needle, than for a rich man to enter into the
> kingdom of God" (Mark 10:25).

I have read the New Testament over and over and have focused on the words of Jesus Christ, and what I have found is warning after warning to repent and turn away from sin, all sin. Also, to be awake, watchful, sober, and expecting Jesus to return any time. In other words, live your life each day as though you are prepared to die and meet Jesus. Someone once asked me, what sin can stop me from going to heaven? And my answer to that question is, all the sins that you refuse to repent of because you love the sin more than you love God. First of all, if you don't read the Bible, you may not realize how sinful your life really is. That is why God gave us His Word so we will not walk in darkness. Then God gave us His son, Jesus, so we can be forgiven and receive power to overcome all sin and temptation. I know it's not easy, but Jesus knows how we struggle, and he is an ever- present help even in our darkest hour.

Satan's big lie is this: you don't have to change because you were born that way. The truth is, we were all born into a state of sin and all are in need of a savior. Acts 4:12 says, "Neither is there salvation in any other: for there is none other name under heaven given among men, whereby we must be saved." The name that is above all names is Jesus Christ. If you truly repent, then you will ask Jesus to show you daily what sins are in your life and ask for the strength to turn away from sin and the power to say no to Satan and his bag of tricks. You will know when you are right with God because Jesus will confirm it with your spirit. You will know that you know that you know. "Be ye holy for I am holy, saith the Lord!"

Only One Way to Heaven

> "Verily, verily, I say unto you, He that enters not by the door into the sheepfold, but has climbed up some other way, the same is a thief and a robber" (John 10:1).

People are living carelessly today, but there is a day coming in the not too distant future when all hell will break loose. Jesus warns us that in the last days before He returns, there will be great tribulation, worse than any other time that the world has ever seen. You can read about it in the gospel of Matthew chapter 24.

There will be more earthquakes, more powerful and more frequent. There will be more volcanoes, meteors, and category 5 storms. There will be civil unrest, killings, and looting. There will be food shortages, famine, and deadly diseases, and pandemics. Many false prophets and false Christs will appear worldwide. People will be misled, and many will reject sound doctrine. There will be a great falling away; people will stop going to church. Many churches will close due to lack of funds. True Christian believers will meet in homes, often in secret due to persecution. But when the Lord Jesus returns to judge the world, many will run and hide. Some will say "Lord, Lord" and pretend to be Christians. That is when the Lord will say, "I never knew you: depart from me, ye that work iniquity" (Matt.7:23).

You cannot save yourselves by good works. Even if you did many good works in your life, if you deny Christ, you are destined to go to hell. There is only one way to heaven, and that is through Jesus Christ. After you accept Jesus and make Him Lord of your life, then show Him how much you love Him by *doing* His commandments. They are not His suggestions.

Some people think that by being a member of a church or organization or a political movement or human rights organization that God will respect that and let them into heaven. That is simply not true. The Bible says in the book of Acts 10:34, "Then Peter opened his mouth, and said, 'Of a truth I perceive that God is no respecter of persons.'" You can be a king, a queen, or president, but that will not get you special treatment on judgment day. One day we will have to stand before God and be judged. On that day God will open the books to review how we lived our lives. Then God will open the book of life, also known as the Lamb's Book of Life, to see if your name has been written in the book. This is the book where you want your name to be written. The only way to have your name written in the Book of Life is to be born again. "Jesus answered and said unto him, 'Verily, verily, I say unto thee, except a man be born again, he cannot see the kingdom of God'" (John 3:3). Once your name is written in the book of life, pray that you never backslide to the point of having your name blotted out (Ps. 69:28 and Rev. 22:19).

The best position a person could be in when the Lord returns is on your knees in prayer, praying to the Father in the name of his Son, Jesus Christ. It is a good habit to get into. Don't put it off; you may never get another chance. They say if there were a nuclear attack we might have a twenty-minute warning. What would you do in your last twenty minutes before you die? You can't fool God. He knows what your motives are and if you have a hidden agenda. Don't fool yourself into thinking that you will live in sin and then repent on your deathbed or fall down on your knees when He returns in glory. I believe there is a cutoff point and an appointed time that only God knows, and once that point in time is reached, it will be too late to repent. I base my findings on a Bible verse that is right before Jesus returns. Revelation 22:11 states, "He that is unjust, let him be unjust still: and he which is filthy, let him be filthy still: and he that is righteous, let him be righteous still: and he that is holy, let him be holy still."

The Revolution

> "If my people, which are called by my name, shall humble themselves and pray and seek my face, and turn from their wicked ways, then will I hear from heaven, and will forgive their sins and will heal their land" (2 Chron. 7:14).

There are multiple millions of people in American that call themselves Christians. Many have believed a lie from hell that they can live for the devil and still be saved. They have compromised their morals and have defiled themselves with the filth of the world. These same people complain about the direction and moral decline of our country, but they don't see themselves as a part of the problem. People of America, wake up! It's time for a revolution! It's time to take back our nation! Not by violence, but by personal holiness.

Look inward to your own soul and repent. This holiness is only obtained when we are aware of the holiness of Jesus and we ask him to come and live in us.

I am talking about a spiritual revolution such as this country has never seen. A spiritual revolution that will dictate what the future of America will be. If only the Christians could unite under one common banner, "Personal Holiness," and glorify our Lord, Jesus Christ, in every aspect of our lives. This will be a personal choice that would change not only America, but the world!

Writing this book, *The Narrow Path*, has changed my life for the better. It is my hope that after you read this book you will have a spiritual renewal. The Revelation will give birth to the revolution.

My Vision for America

One by one they will turn from their wicked ways, refusing to go to the movies that are an abomination; refusing to go to the liquor stores, barrooms, casinos; refusing to support abortions and violence in books, TV, internet, movies; refusing pornography in all forms; refusing to support the churches that do not preach God's Word. We should support the pastors that have the guts to call sin, sin. But it all has to start on a personal level. One by one, until God heals our land, where our children and grandchildren can live in peace and safety, where the evil is cast out and replaced with the words "America - One Nation under God in Christ JESUS!"

Let *His* Name be inscribed on every government building and every church. Our founding fathers went wrong when they said, "In God we trust." They omitted the name Jesus Christ. Many of our founding fathers were Masons. There are many false gods in the world. What god did they worship?

Run from the Devil!

"And a stranger will they not follow, but will flee from him; for they know not the voice of strangers" (John 10:5).

"Flee also youthful lusts; but follow righteousness, faith, charity, peace, with them that call on the Lord out of a pure heart" (2 Tim. 2:22).

In war there are many battles; and there is a time to attack, a time to hold your ground, and a time to retreat. I want to focus on when it is time to retreat from the devil. I pray you will know when to run from the agents of Satan that very often work through people.

"Flee fornication. Every sin that a man doeth is without the body; but he that commits fornication sins against his own body" (1 Cor. 6:18).

When you first accept Jesus, you are a new babe in Christ. Like a baby, you need to be weaned on the milk of the Word. In the beginning of your walk with Jesus, He doesn't expect you, as a babe, to grab the sword of the Spirit and get in a sword fight with demons. This is only for the most mature Christian warriors. Believe me, you wouldn't last five minutes against the skills of Satan. Remember that Satan has been around since before Adam and Eve. He has destroyed many strong men and women throughout history. So, while you are learning the Word of God and praying for strength to overcome the enemy, you need to learn when to run from the devil.

First, you need to read the Word and learn what is good and what is evil. Then you need to pray for a hedge of protection around your life. Everyone's circumstances are different, so you have to look at where you are and do a personal assessment of what area the devil has used as an access point into your life before you can plan your retreat. If you are deep into alcohol and drugs, then you can do several things. The first thing is to tell all your contacts that you are a born-again Christian and you want to change your life. After you do that, you will know who your real friends are and those that are being used by Satan to bring you down. The second thing to do is to change your phone number so they will not be able to call you to tempt you to do drugs. If that doesn't work, then you need to plan your escape. Don't tell anyone but those you trust that you plan to move. Move to a different location and cut ties with everyone that drinks and does drugs, even family members. If you need help for your addictions, *Teen Challenge* has a good success rate.

Now you can start a new life and get into a church group that can offer some spiritual support in the areas that you struggle with. Remember that God knows you and your struggle and He will help you by sending the Holy Spirit to give you peace and strength and wisdom.

The best way to know Jesus is by reading the Bible. Start at Matthew and read what Jesus said. Most Bibles highlight quotations of Jesus in red letters. Put on the mind of Christ and apply His teachings to your life. If you do this, you will feel a pull to go to church and to serve in His kingdom. You will also seek to walk the narrow path that few ever find. Few find this narrow path because they are not willing to crucify their flesh and repent.

Sexual Sin

"The people of Sodom and Gomorrah gave themselves over to fornication, adultery, homosexuality and only God knows what else! These two cities were destroyed by fire by two angels sent from God. This was an example of God's judgment, and one way He deals with sin. The only reason that God hasn't destroyed America yet is because there are many good Christians living here. In Sodom and Gomorrah, the angels said they would not destroy them if they could find just ten good people. The only people that were saved were Lot and his family. And Lot's wife was turned into a pillar of salt because she didn't heed the warning, to not look back. That is why it is important for us, to not look back at our old life with a desire to return to our sinful ways that God has delivered us from" (Jude 7).

> "Likewise also these filthy dreamers defile the flesh, despise dominion and speak evil of dignities" (Jude 8).

Look around you at the condition of our society. The people are blinded to the depths of depravity in which our nation has fallen. If eyes could see into the spiritual realm, millions would run to the churches for deliverance from evil. Millions would run to the churches in repentance. But, because they have chosen to serve Satan and their flesh, they have rejected Jesus Christ as Lord over their lives. People run to money, sex, drugs, rock and roll, sports, etc.; but you practically have to drag people to church.

> "And I gave her space to repent of her fornications; and she repented not. Behold, I will cast her into a bed and them that commit adultery with her into great tribulation, except they repent of their deeds" (Rev. 2:21, 22).
> "And rend your heart and not your garments, and turn unto the Lord your God; for He is gracious and merciful, slow to anger, and of great kindness, and repents of the evil" (Joel 2:13)

Here we have the prophet Joel talking about "rending" (ripping or tearing) the clothing, which was done by the Jews as an outward sign of grieving over sin or loss. Sometimes it's easier to display our distress by an outward sign rather than getting to the root of the problem, which many times comes from the heart.

We are all like children when it comes to being obedient to God. But, when God reveals to us His holiness and we get serious, that is when we realize how we fall short of God's expectations.

This is why God gives us space. The space is a certain length of time. This is a time of grace or a grace period. This is a call to repentance and holiness, a call to purify our soul from evil.

Choose Wisely

Every time we choose to sin when the Holy Spirit tells us not to, we are telling God, no! Just like a child that is disobedient to mother or father and when told to do something, the child says no! Now, just as the parent is loving and patient toward their child, so is God with us.

Some people have lots of issues, and some have had extremely hard times growing up. Some have addictions and mental problems, but the good news is that Jesus has provided a way for all to find their way out of the forest and onto the narrow path that leads to everlasting life.

Everyone is given a space of time to repent. The important thing is for us to never stop repenting when we fall into sin. When we stop repenting, then we are telling God, "No, I am not sorry for my sins" and that is a very dangerous place to be for God is not done with you yet. To be chastised by the hand of God is a terrible position to find yourself in.

God will not be mocked. He doesn't play games. This is serious business, and it is important to realize that God is in control of everything, from the rising of the sun to the spider on the wall. You can't run and you can't hide from the hand of God's power.

What Is God's Will?

> "Because strait is the gate and narrow is the way which leadeth unto life and few there be that find it" (Matt. 7:14).

It is God's will for us to be obedient to His commandments; to accept His only begotten son, Jesus Christ; and to go to church and fellowship with other Christians. It is God's will that we support the church, receive communion, give offerings to the poor, support missionaries, visit the sick, help the widows and orphans. It is God's will we give our personal testimony to strangers and to help spread God's word to the lost and to the world. It is God's will we stay faithful to our spouse, our country, our church, our family. That we speak the truth and help our family through the bad times as well as the good times. We must gently guide our children in the paths of righteousness by showing love and patience. We must lead by example, not by mere words alone. We must be a shoulder to lean on and cry on if needed. We must be quick to help, slow to anger, willing to be humble and not prideful. We must forgive those that have done us wrong, as we would have them forgive us.

We need to put ourselves in another's shoes, to try to understand where that person is coming from and how to meet their needs. We need to pray for wisdom and protection from the enemy. We need to daily examine ourselves to keep from sin.

We need to know who we are in Christ and not be ashamed of Jesus. We need to stand firm and not waiver or be tossed about like a boat in a storm. We need to be unshaken and unwilling to be moved off the rock of Christ. We need to be rooted deeply and have faith that there is only one way to heaven and that is through Jesus Christ, the only door to reach the Father.

We need to be purified with fire, by resisting temptations to sin and by being victorious over sin. Each time we win a spiritual battle, we become stronger and closer to God. Each time we step on the head of the serpent, Satan, we see more of the things of the Spirit and the veils are removed from our eyes. We can then see our destiny as we walk the narrow path. If we stay on God's path, we will be spared from the evil and destruction that could have been our destiny had we followed after the path of sin.

The Chosen

> "If ye were of the world, the world would love his own; but because ye are not of the world, but I have chosen you out of the world, therefore the world hates you" (John 15:19).

What Jesus is saying here is that the world, or the majority of the people of the world, will in fact, reject Christianity. Why? Because they are of the world, the worldly system of things. The majority are evil. They lust after money, power, sex, materialism, sinful lifestyles; and because of their lifestyles of ungodliness, many are rewarded with wealth. For some, Satan rewards those that follow him but the end result is unhappiness, misery, and death, followed by eternal damnation. The world is full of lost souls wandering in a forest full of sin.

If you have truly accepted Christ and chose to walk the narrow path, then rejoice in the fact that He chose you! He called you out of a world that lives in darkness.

Now the reason the world hates Jesus Christ and you as a Christian is because Christ in you will expose evil and sin to the world. The world would rather have no laws restricting their evil intentions.

Look at what happened to John the Baptist. He prepared the way for Jesus by calling sinners to repent and be baptized. He told King Herod that it was unlawful for him to take his brother's wife, and he was imprisoned. As a result of John pointing our Herod's sin, Herod's unlawful wife plotted with her daughter to seduce Herod with a dance and then ask for the head of John the Baptist on a platter. It was done all because of sin being exposed.

> "For yourselves know perfectly that the day of the Lord so cometh as a thief in the night... But ye, brethren, are not in darkness that that day should overtake you as a thief. Ye are all the children of light and the children of the day; we are not of the night nor of darkness. Therefore, let us not sleep, as do others; but let us watch and be sober" (1 Thess. 5:2 and 5:4–6).

There is coming a day in everyone's life when they will suddenly realize that death is near. There is also coming a day when Jesus Christ will return with a shout. Either way, you have to ask, Am I ready to meet the Lord?

This is why it is of utmost importance for the Christian to purify themselves. Take a moral inventory of your life, and deal with any sin in your life. This is no small matter. Whenever a person turns to Christ and repents, the angels rejoice and the demons howl and scream. The end result is a state of being where you can look at yourself in the mirror and say, "I am ready to meet my Lord, Jesus Christ." This is a great place to be: spiritually ready.

Let's face it, many Christians are asleep and walking in darkness. If Christ was to return today or if there was a nuclear attack and it came as a thief in the night, many would not be ready. This is due to many reasons. One reason some Christians are living in sin is because (1) they are not being taught properly in church; (2) they have been taught by an immoral system of the public schools; (3) they have been taught by liberals with Antichristian bias, to say the least, and some teach many to hold higher education up on a pedestal as being higher than the moral teachings of the Bible; (4) some are aware of their sins but feel too weak to overcome the temptations; (5) some are aware of their sins but are not convicted by the Holy Spirit, so they don't feel the urgency to repent or they may have never received the baptism of the Holy Spirit; (6) some have allowed the devil to build a stronghold in their thoughts; (7) some are involved with the dark side to the point of demonic possession; and (8) some Christians believe it is not necessary to repent in order to be saved, as some believe that baptism is not required. This is being lazy, unresponsive, and shows a lack of being committed to Christ.

Some of you are thinking, *Jesus died for my sins, so I don't have to worry if I am living in sin.* Not true! Remember when God delivered the Israelites out of Egypt and Moses parted the Red Sea and drowned the pursuing Egyptians? God heard their prayers and led the captives into freedom victoriously. But when Moses was receiving the Ten Commandments from God while he was on the mountain, the people made an idol and got drunk and fell into sin and had a big party. Well, when Moses came down from the mountain, he told the people to choose sides and God destroyed about half of those that were just saved by His power. This is a reminder to Christians to not feel as though you cannot lose your salvation. Jude 1:5 says, "I will therefore put you in remembrance, though ye once knew this, how that the Lord, having saved the people out of Egypt, afterward destroyed them that believed not."

Every Knee Will Bow

God is holy, Jesus is holy, so it is God's will that we be holy. If you are wondering what is God's will for your life, then wonder no more. The first and utmost will of God for you and I is to seek to be purified by His Holiness, to walk the narrow path, and to turn away from all ungodliness. Examine and judge yourself daily so you will not be ashamed on the great and terrible Day of the Lord when every knee will bow and every tongue will confess that Jesus Christ is Lord of all.

> "Greater love hath no man than this, that a man lay down his life for his friends" (John 15:13).
> "The Lord is a man of war, the Lord is His Name" (Exod. 15:3). "And I will execute great vengeance upon them with furious rebukes; and they shall know that I am the Lord, when I shall lay my vengeance upon them" (Ezek. 25:17).

War is a terrible thing and should be avoided if possible. That is why Jesus died for us, to show mankind a better way to coexist in a world of different beliefs. He also came to show us how to battle our inner war, the spirit against the flesh.

There are enemies within and enemies without. The enemies within, we can fight with the Word of God to the perfecting of our souls. The enemies without, we are to win over with love for Jesus said we are to love our enemies.

But there is another enemy without that hates everything that is good. This enemy pretends to be godly but their heart is full of hatred toward the things of God. They hate freedom and liberty and the American way. This enemy will burn the American flag and trample our freedoms. They live a lie. They say they are holy and do God's will; yet they kill innocent men, women, and children. To them, life is cheap. They value nothing. They oppress their women and enclave their children. They are willing to kill themselves as a way to kill others. They are totally brainwashed by Satan to hate and kill anyone that gets in their way, especially Christians and Jews. Why Christians and Jews? Because they know that God is with the Christians and the Jews, and they hate God.

This war is nothing new. It has been raging for thousands of years. What is important is to choose sides. Who will you fight for?

God hates a coward. If you serve the true God, you will be willing to love your enemies as Jesus taught us.

But there may come a time when you will have to fight to protect your family and friends and the American way of freedom that we all enjoy. These freedoms we enjoy are ours because of the servicemen and women that served in our military and some fought and died for us. Without those brave men and women, we would not have the freedoms we hold dear to our hearts. America, one nation, under God, with liberty and justice for all.

Sin in the Land

> "Son of man, when the land sins against me by *trespassing* grievously, then I will stretch out mine hand upon it, and will break the staff of the bread thereof, and will send famine upon it and will cut off man and beast from it" (Ezek. 14:13).
>
> "And you hath he quickened, who were dead in *trespasses* and sins, Wherein in time past ye walked according to the course of this world, according to the prince of the power of the air, the spirit that now worketh in the children of disobedience" (Eph. 2:1, 2).

Trespass means (1) to exceed the bounds of what is lawful, right or just; to sin; to offend. (2) hence, to encroach, as on another's privileges, rights, privacy, etc.; to intrude.

America has grievously trespassed the laws of God. Our leaders have judged wrongly. They call good evil and evil good. They have changed the laws to legalize sin that for centuries was illegal. What was once holy is now forgotten and replaced by the teachings of men and women. The land is full of false teachers and false prophets. Our Supreme Court justices have become people pleasers, ruling in favor of the latest popular opinions, with a partisan bias and a total disrespect for the rule of law, which had its roots in the Bible. "Professing themselves to be wise, they became fools" (Rom. 1:22).

The Lord will return for His church, a church without spot or wrinkle. Now is the time, past time, for every Christian to purify themselves. Every thought, deed, and intention needs to be purified.

Do not be deceived by the false prophets. Repent, repent, America, repent! Soon there will be such sorrows as the world has never known. Our only hope will be to be taken up in the Rapture of the church of Christ. The Bible describes the church as the bride of Christ. Jesus will not take a whore as His bride. The true church of Christ is not confined to church denominations or religious doctrine. There will be a gathering and a catching away, a great harvest of the earth. Those that have washed their garments in the blood of Christ and have attained spiritual purity, to be without spot or wrinkle, those will be taken out of the world and translated to the incorruptible body of Christ. We shall meet the Lord in the air as we move toward the heavenly home that Christ has prepared for those that love and obey His commandments. All others will be left behind to suffer His wrath in the days of tribulation. Many will be saved during the seven-year tribulation, but they will have to be tested. To prove their faith, many will be martyred, many by beheading, as described in the book of Revelation 20:4, "And I saw the souls of them that were beheaded for the witness of Jesus..."

Signs of the End

> "And as he sat upon the Mount of Olives, the disciples came unto Him privately saying, 'Tell us, when shall these things be? And what shall be the sign of thy coming, and of the end of the world'" (Matt. 24:3).

The following is a list of signs that indicate we are living in the last generation that Jesus talked about. He said all these signs together will be accomplished in that last generation. They will see Jesus return in a monumental grand entrance, riding on the clouds of heaven, for all people to see. He also warns us not to follow after false Christs that will appear here or there. When the true Jesus returns, it will be like the lightning that flashes from east to west.

These signs to look for are from the four Gospels, Matthew, Mark, Luke, and John:

Many false Christs or false teachings

1. Wars and rumors of wars
2. Nations will rise against nation
3. Kingdom against kingdom
4. Famines, pestilences, earthquakes
5. These are the beginning of sorrows
6. Persecution of Christians worldwide
7. Christians will be killed
8. People will be easily offended
9. People will be hateful
10. People will betray one another
11. Many false prophets will arise and deceive
12. And evil will increase
13. Love will decrease
14. The gospel will be preached to all nations
15. The abomination of desolation spoken of in the book of Daniel.
16. A time to flee to safety
17. Woe to women that are pregnant or nursing their babies
18. Pray that your flight is not during winter or on the Sabbath
19. There will be great tribulation such as the world has never seen before or ever will again.
20. So great a tribulation that if those days had not been cut short, no flesh will be saved.
21. The sun will be darkened and the moon will not give its light and the stars of heaven will fall and the powers of heaven will be shaken.
22. Then the Lord will return.
23. Other signs to look for:

Distress of nations, with perplexity

1. Men's hearts failing for fear
2. Sea and waves roaring
3. Fearful sights and great signs in the heavens
4. Betrayals within families, children having parents put to death.

Draw close to Jesus. He will be your peace.

I Believe

I believe in the risen Christ. His name is Jesus, and He lives. His power can make me whole again. His holiness shines a light in my soul. His love is everlasting. His mercy can reach the lost sheep. He will never forsake me. When I sin, that is my failure. When I sin, I am in rebellion. When I sin, I am running from Christ. When I sin, I am moving from life to death. Lord Jesus, save me from my sins. I repent, Lord Jesus, make me whole. Keep me from all evil, save me from this world of sin. I have failed to live a life worthy of your high standards. Strengthen me in my daily walk. Let your life's light shine on me every minute of every day and be with me through the darkness of night as a light from a candle whose wax never melts and no shadow is cast.

Lord Jesus, I want to be ready when that trumpet blows to every corner of the earth. Please, Lord Jesus, sanctify me in my body, mind, and spirit so I will be raptured and not left behind. Amen.

God's Seal

"Labor not for the meat which perisheth, but for that meat which endureth unto everlasting life, which the Son of man shall give unto you: for him hath God the Father sealed" (John 6:27).

In the old days a king would have a signet ring or a royal seal; and whatever the king decreed as a law or a letter, he would make an impression on that document with his seal, usually pressed in hot wax. Everyone knew that if that decree had the king's seal on it, no one but the king could change it.

Once you are truly born again and are on the narrow path of seeking and serving Christ, Jesus will give you spiritual meat for your soul to digest. You can trust every word that Jesus spoke, as written in the Bible, as the Word of God, the Father. Why? Because God the Father sent his Son, Jesus, and Jesus has been sealed by God. Because Jesus has been sealed, we can take every word that Jesus said as God's decree, God's laws, God's commandments. There is no other religion or way of man that has God's seal. Only Christ was worthy enough to be sealed.

All these other man-made religions are fake, phony, counterfeits. Some will say they follow the Bible, but they will say they have more books or something new to add, one that has more importance than the Bible. There are also many cults that distort the gospel. They may present themselves as being from God, but are wolves in sheep's clothing! Don't be fooled! That is why it is of the utmost importance to study and know the Bible for yourself. If you don't know what the Bible says, you will set yourself up to join a cult. And there are many cults in America. I could list a few, but I won't. Everyone needs to do some research and pray that Jesus will direct their steps.

I believe the King James Bible is God's word to man. However, I would compare the four gospels to be that meat that Jesus refers to in John 6:27 and the rest of the New Testament as mashed potatoes and gravy and Old Testament books as vegetables with Psalms as desert. All put together, the Bible makes a wonderful meal for the soul.

The world is full of false gods, and as a result, the world is full of false teachers and false religions. This is because man would rather create his own god, a god that allows man to sin.

How many of these world religions have God the Father's holy seal? Who else other than Jesus who lived, was recorded in history, died for all to see on the cross, was buried, rose from the dead, back to life on the third day, with power and glory; was seen alive again by over five hundred eyewitnesses, and was seen ascending into heaven before their very eyes. Even the years are numbered around the birth and death of Jesus Christ. BC and AD (Before Christ and After Death).

The Chosen

> "For many are called, but few are chosen" (Matt.
> 22:14)."Ye have not chosen me, but I have cho-
> sen you, and ordained you, that ye should go
> and bring forth fruit, and that your fruit should
> remain: that whatsoever ye shall ask of the Father
> in my name, He may give it you" (John 15:16).

It is not God's will that anyone perish, but He gave us free will to choose what path we will walk in life. Therefore, many perish because they reject Christ and serve the devil, whether they realize it or not.

Many are called to repentance, and many do seek God's king-dom, but only as an afterthought or enough to barely be saved. Some only go to church to get free handouts such as free food, money, help for their family problems, home repairs, weddings, funerals, etc. And after they get what they want, they don't come back. These are the same people that will call the faithful church members hypocrites.

Some diligently seek God and study the Bible. By their own free will they do this. Then one day God's Spirit speaks to their spirit, and at that point, they become chosen by God and enter the ministry. If their motive is to serve and not to be served for greedy financial gain, then God will use that person for His Kingdom. There are too many preachers that use God as a business investment.

God observes what we choose to do with our free will. And depending on our purpose and our heart, Jesus adds His grace to guide us according to His purpose that we may serve Him. There is no higher calling than to serve God.

To Err Is Death to the Soul

> "Brethren, if any of you do err from the truth,
> and one convert him; Let him know, that he
> which converts the sinner from the error of his
> way shall save a soul from death, and shall hide

a multitude of sins" (James 5:19, 20). *Err* means to fall into error; to go astray; especially, to do wrong, to sin.

Convert implies a hearty, usually genuine embracing of a creed, opinion or doctrine previously rejected or at least not accepted.

Everyone wants to be saved, but few are willing to convert. Many Christian churches are in error. James is addressing the brethren, which implies that many were following false doctrine within the church.

We are blessed today to have the Bible available to us. The early church had few copies of the Written Word. Most teachings were by word of mouth, preaching. The problem today is a lot of churches have become social clubs. Many have stopped preaching and teaching the basics.

The first doctrine to go by the wayside is paying the tithe. Although the tithe is a biblical principle, I don't believe it is necessary for the church in America at the present time. The reason is, we have been blessed with so many social safety nets that have been around since after the Great Depression of the last century. Before there were all these government programs to help the poor, the churches were the primary helpers and the tithe was required of all Christians but not forced. All charitable giving has to come from the heart and not because someone compels you to give more than you can afford to give. This happens a lot when people use the television as their church. In the end they make somebody wealthy beyond their wildest imagination.

Don't search the Bible for a legal loophole that will exempt you from turning away from sin. If you do, you are in error from the truth. We should all search the Bible to find out what is pleasing to God and do those things and then search what is sinful and angers God and purge those things from our lives. Now this should be our goal in life. Put God first, ahead of all things. If you do, your light will shine. Praise God!

My Soul

Lord Jesus, your Word is a lamp unto my feet.

Lord, help me to not stumble along the path of life. As Satan tries to trip me, your Word will show me every obstacle the devil puts on my path.

Lord Jesus, You are the Holy One. Your Glory lights my path and my very soul. Your light is so complete; it shines and illuminates every corner, leaving sin no shadow to hide in.

Lord Jesus, your Word can lead the lost out of the wilderness and your Light can set the captive free. Amen.

Jesus Sends

"Go ye therefore, and teach all nations, baptizing them in the name of the Father, and of the Son, and of the Holy Ghost: Teaching them to observe all things whatsoever I have commanded you: and, lo, I am with you always, even unto the end of the world. Amen" (Matt. 28:19–20).

"And whosoever shall not receive you, nor hear you, when ye depart thence, shake off the dust under your feet for a testimony against them. Verily I say unto you, it shall be more tolerable for Sodom and Gomorrah in the Day of Judgment than for that city" (Mark 6:11).

"Jesus sends forth the twelve apostles, two by two, and gave them power over unclean spirits" (Mark 6:7).

"And they went out and preached that men should repent. And they cast out many devils, and anointed with oil many that were sick and healed them" (Mark 6:12, 13).

Jesus and His apostles went about the country, preaching that men should repent, and they healed the sick and cast out devils. Three things:

1. Repent
2. Healing
3. Deliverance

Yet some didn't receive them and didn't want to hear the gospel message. Why? These are all good things. Why wouldn't everyone want to be free of devils, healed of sickness, repent of sins, and be close to God? Why do some hear preaching while others reject it?

If you preach repentance from sin, you touch a raw nerve with those that are living in sin. They don't want to hear that kind of a message because they know that they would have to change the way they live. In other words, they would have to stop sinning and they derive pleasure and profit from their sins.

But there is a different type of preaching they will listen to and that is the preacher that preaches an easy message: a message of love and acceptance; of love thyself and if it feels good, do it; there is no hell or punishment; there are many paths that all lead to the same place; or don't judge, just accept everyone and everything with love.

The reason they listen to these false preachers is to justify living in sin and to have someone to point the finger to on Judgment Day and say to God, "It was that preacher that taught me that way."

But no matter what, they will not be able to stand on Judgment Day due to the fact that they were not willing to repent of their sins. They didn't want to face the true God of the Bible. The Old Testament laws were tough, but Jesus was tougher on sin than all the Old Testament prophets. Amen.

Listen

Listen carefully to what the Lord says.
Seek the Holy Spirit while you can.
Do not grieve the Holy Spirit.

Beware of the unpardonable sin (rejecting Jesus, refusing the Holy Spirit).

You are not an orphan. You are grafted into the True Vine. You are a member of the great and glorious Body of Christ.

Therefore, walk with the Spirit in a manner that is worthy of a child of God. If you feel like an orphan and you live to follow the flesh, the world, and the devil, then repent! Repent! Turn away from all evil. Be baptized and seek God, Jesus, and the Holy Spirit while the Spirit may still be found. We are living in a time of blessings and curses. Evil is increasing, but so is God's grace. Set your feet on the narrow path and set your spiritual compass to point towards heaven. The body of Christ is heaven bound. For this world and everything in it shall pass away in the great and terrible Day of the Lord. Amen.

A New Creature

> "But God forbid that I should glory, save in the cross of our Lord Jesus Christ, by whom the world is crucified unto me and I unto the world. For in Christ Jesus neither circumcision availed anything nor uncircumcision, but a new creature" (Gal. 6:14, 15).
>
> "Therefore, if any man be in Christ, he is a new creature: old things are passed away; behold, all things are become new" (2 Cor. 5:17).

Did you know that when you accepted Jesus Christ as your savior, you became a new creature? Yes, at that moment, you said the sinner's prayer and asked Jesus into your heart. That is when the transformation began. Do you have enough faith to believe what is written in the Bible? Or do you doubt the power of Christ? Jesus said, "I am the Resurrection." He wasn't resurrected by some external power; He resurrected himself because He is the power.

The true Christians have been transformed into a new creature, whether they know it or not. Some are like the caterpillar, coming out of the cocoon as a beautiful butterfly. The problem is, some don't know they are butterflies yet, and instead of flapping their wings to fly, they still walk along the branch with their little legs.

Now what would have happened to the apostle Paul if after seeing Christ on the road to Damascus, he said, "I am born again. I think I will expand my tent-making business and make a lot of money and see how much material blessing the Lord will bless me with. I won't persecute Christians anymore. I will be good, but I just won't make any waves. After all, I don't want to be persecuted like them, so I will keep a low profile and be blessed. I will keep it to myself. All the Christians will know how blessed I am by how much money I will make in my new tent business."

No! Paul chose to flap his wings as a new creature in Christ and wrote most of the New Testament in the Bible. It wasn't any easy life for Paul, but he has great rewards in heaven. Paul tells us the hardships that he suffered for following Jesus and staying on the narrow path. Paul was whipped five times, receiving thirty-nine lashes each time.

> "Of the Jews five times received I forty stripes save one. Thrice was I beaten with rods, once was I stoned, thrice I suffered shipwreck, a night and a day I have been in the deep" (2 Cor. 11:24, 25).

Lord, give us faith enough to become the new creature and live in Your will, not our will. Amen.

God's Word

> "Thy Word is a lamp unto my feet, and a light unto my path" (Ps. 119:105).

You wake up, get dressed, and read God's Word. What a wonderful way to start the day!

> "Teach me Thy way, O Lord, and lead me in a plain path, because of my enemies" (Ps. 27:11).

The days are evil. We have enemies, even in our own houses. They try to steal our peace, our joy in the Lord. But God's hedge of protection won't let that happen.

> "And a man's foes shall be they of his own household" (Matt. 10:36).

Sunshine and blue skies are a gift from God. I will enjoy the day and thank God for it while I can.

Afterwards, the night comes and the lamp of God's Word lights my path so I won't stumble and fall. Without God's Word, I am lost in darkness. I would become easy prey for a lion or wolves.

Every day is a new day. Another challenge, another test, another temptation may come our way. And another night follows the day.

> "They that were foolish took their lamps and took no oil with them. Afterward came also the other virgins saying, 'Lord, Lord, open to us." But He answered and said, 'Verily, verily I say unto you, I know you not'" (Matt. 25:3, 11, 12).

Jesus gives us the parable of the ten virgins: five were wise and five were foolish. The wise brought oil for their lamps; the foolish did not. The wise entered into the kingdom of God; the foolish did not.

How can we apply this parable to our lives? If God's Word is a lamp to our path, then to have our life illuminated by God, we need to read the Bible every day to be prepared spiritually. Just like when the power goes out in a storm and you know you have flashlights, but you can't find one or you find a flashlight but the batteries are dead. If Jesus gave this parable in the context of today, He would have said, the five foolish women brought no spare batteries for their flashlights.

So keep plenty of spare fresh batteries for your flashlights by reading God's Word daily and apply it to your life. We need to be ready when our Lord returns. Also, we need to be ready every day; we don't know when we will die. Remember the twin towers on 9/11.

Jesus's Suffering

> "And he taketh with him Peter and James and John, and began to be sore amazed, and to be very heavy; And saith unto them, My soul is exceeding sorrowful unto death: tarry ye here, and watch" (Mark 14:33–36)

And he went forward a little, and fell on the ground, and prayed that if it were possible, the hour might pass from him. And he said, "Abba, Father, all things are possible unto thee; take away this cup from me: nevertheless not what I will, but what thou wilt."

To understand sin, repentance, forgiveness and sin, unrepentance and hell, you have to understand the concept and meaning of Jesus having to die on the cross. It was not an easy thing for the Son of God, but the Father required the Son to suffer greatly for us. And this is why the Father is justified when he sends sinners to hell. If life was not easy for Jesus, why should life be easy for us? Are we more valuable than Jesus was to the Father?

How can mankind expect to go to heaven, where Jesus is, if they reject the cross of Christ in this life? Is man able to change the will of God if His perfect Son could not? Read Luke 22:42

When I look at the cross, I see two possibilities: (1) I see my salvation made possible by Jesus being the sacrifice, and (2) I see God the Father above that would not spare His son because of sin, not His sin but the sins of the world. John 3:16 says, "For God so loved the world, that He gave His only begotten Son, that whosoever believeth in Him should not perish, but have everlasting life." Because of God's firm foundation and His unchanging character, there must be a change, as evidence of true repentance. You can fool yourself, but you can't fool God. He knows your every thought.

> "And there appeared an angel unto him from heaven, strengthening him. And being in an agony, he prayed more earnestly: and his sweat

was as it were great drops of blood falling down
to the ground" (Luke 22: 43, 44).

Jesus suffered greatly for the world of lost sinners. Billions of people could be saved if they only would repent and walk with Jesus on the narrow path.

Hope

Where does your hope lie? Do you have hope in the grave, to rest in peace for eternity? If so, you are deceived.

You need to repent and receive the living Hope. His name is Jesus Christ, and He will give you a hope that is alive and active here and now.

There is no death, only moving from one place to another. Blink your eyes and you are there. Jesus said, "If you believe in Me, you will never die" God does not reward those that are living in a continual state of sin, whose only hope is in the grave. They deceive themselves because they are a slave to sin by their own lusts because they love their sins more than they love God.

If our good works are as filthy rags to God, then what are our sins like? Does He turn his head away in disgust? Who is your God? Is he a jolly old man in a red suit that says, "Ho, ho, ho, what do you want for Christmas?" Or is your God, the Great I Am, that spoke to the children of Israel through Moses and to Pharaoh, saying, "Let my people go." My hope is in Jesus, the Great I Am.

Feed My Sheep

"For the time is come that judgment must begin at the house of God: and if it first begin with us, what shall the end be of them that obey not the gospel of God? And if the righteous scarcely be saved, where shall the ungodly and the sinner appear?" (1 Pet. 4:17, 18).

"But it is happened unto them according to the true proverb, the dog is turned to his own vomit again; and the sow that is washed to her wallowing in the mire" (2 Pet. 2:22).

Jesus asked Peter three times, "Do you love me?" And Peter replied three times, "Yes, I do!" Then Jesus commanded Peter, saying, "Feed my sheep!"

In the Bible, we have 1 Peter and 2 Peter. Two books within the Bible that deal with sin and how to overcome sin. Peter gives warning after warning to Christians as to the dangers of falling back into the world and the lust of the flesh.

Peter writes about God's judgment beginning in the house of God and then to the world. The house of God are all those that confess or profess to be Christians. Then God will judge those that do not believe the gospel of Christ. Which category are you in?

Then in verse 18, Peter divides those in three more categories: the righteous, the ungodly, and the sinner. Which category do you fall in?

The righteous are those that profess Christ, go to church, support the church with tithes and offerings, and are not ashamed to help spread the gospel, always seeking to improve themselves by studying the Bible and to be more like Christ by His love. The righteous in Jesus Christ don't go around pointing the finger at people that are living in sin and saying, "That person is going to hell." Even though it seems obvious that may be true, we are to pray for that person and, if at all possible, to skillfully but lovingly guide them toward the Narrow Path.

The ungodly are those that want nothing to do with the things of God. They may seem like good people, but they stand for their own accomplishments in life, and they view Christianity as nothing to be desired or foolishness.

"For the preaching of the cross is to them that perish foolishness; but unto us that are saved it is the power of God" (1 Cor. 1:8).

The sinner could be a person from either category, that is to say a person professes to be a Christian but has never repented from their sinful nature, and they creep into the church to defile the true children of God. These are wolves in sheep's clothing. The sinner is also very much prevalent in abundance in the category of the ungodly. Either way, God stands at the door and knocks. God is patient, not wishing that any should perish, but that all would come to repentance and walk the narrow path that our Lord, Jesus Christ, has for those that love him and keep His commandments.

The Dream

Last night I had a dream. In this dream I was leading a group of children through a forest. I was instructed by someone who was another leader to go to the top of the hill and try to stop the water in the stream from running down the hill by sprinkling a certain powder into the stream. By doing this, the powder would form a dam and stop or slow down the water flow. As we reached the top of the hill, several boys were swimming in the stream. I felt the water by putting my feet in the rocky stream, and the water was ice cold, and I feared for their safety. As I looked around, I saw mighty gusts of wind blowing and picking people off the ground and blowing them around like papers. I then looked in the distant valley below and saw many storms on the horizon like one hundred mini tornadoes. I lead the children through the forest and rocky terrain to a safe place. My spirit was troubled by this dream. (1-5-2010)

Love

"For God so loved the world that He gave His only begotten Son, that whosoever believes in Him shall not perish, but will have everlasting life" (John 3:16).

Do we believe in Jesus? Do you know that the devils believe and tremble at His Name? What about those that perish? That is a frightening thought. But why? What is the true qualifying aspect of this verse?

If you have never professed Jesus Christ as your savior, then you must be on the side with all the people that are going to perish. But what about people that believe that Jesus Christ did exist, historically speaking, or they may even be open to the possibility that He is resurrected and exists in heaven. Isn't that what the demons believe?

> "But wilt thou know, O vain man, that faith without works is dead?" (James 2:20).

Yes, my friend, to truly believe in Jesus Christ is more than that. The Bible says you must be born again. Repent, be baptized as a public display of your faith and obedience, then let the Holy Spirit transform your life by the renewing of your mind. Then you can say with confidence, "I am a born again child of God and a member of the body of Christ and I will live forever in heaven with Jesus."

> "For the Lord himself shall desend from heaven with a shout, with the voice of the archangel, and with the trump of God: and the dead in Christ shall rise first" (1 Thess. 4:16)
>
> "Then we which are alive and remain shall be caught up together with them in the clouds, to meet the Lord in the air; and so shall we ever be with the Lord. Amen" (1 Thess. 4:17).

The Kingdom

The kingdom of God is described in Matthew chapter 13 as something to be desired. Jesus spoke of His kingdom in parables. His disciples asked Jesus to explain the parable of the wheat and the tares, which he did. In verses 44 and 45, the kingdom of God is compared to something of great value, something that is found, and something that the person that found it was willing to sell all they had to obtain it. Then the kingdom of God is compared to a huge net case out and pulled into shore, full of different types of fish. The good fish were kept in vessels, and the bad were cast away.

The Bible gives us many examples of an event occurring in the future of a sorting out or a separating event. To those that were found worthy, to be saved by God, it was a good and glorious day. But to those that were found offensive, it will be the worst day of their lives. The Bible speaks of those as being cast into a furnace of fire, where there will be wailing and gnashing of teeth. Jesus then asked, "Have you understood all these things?" His disciples said, "Yes, Lord."

Walk with Christ

"As ye have, therefore, received Christ Jesus the Lord, so walk ye in Him; Rooted and built up in Him, and established in the faith, as ye have been taught, abounding therein with thanksgiving. Beware lest any man spoil you through philosophy and vain deceit, after the tradition of men, after the rudiments of the world, and not after Christ" (Col. 2:6–8).

If we are not rooted and built up in Christ, the world will try to usurp the position of Christ from our lives by replacing our faith in Jesus with an overexalted view of higher education. There are many men and women that are teaching ungodly doctrines that are mere doctrine of demons disguised as a higher level of learning and understanding, which would replace Jesus Christ as Lord over our lives. The Bible warns us of evil that creeps into our lives and into the church. This is an evil that is easy to recognize. Test the spirits, for not all are from God. If they tell you it's all right to be homosexual or to live in adultery and fornication, then turn away from that teaching because it is an abomination to Christ. Amen.

Endure unto the End

"And ye shall be hated of all men for My name's sake: but he that shall endure unto the end, the same shall be saved" (Mark 13:13).

There has been a lot of talk about how we are living in the last days and how Jesus will return at any time. I believe before Jesus returns, there will be a great falling away from the faith. This will be preceded by persecution of Christians and Jews. I believe that the whole world will believe a big lie. That lie will be that the world's economic collapse will be blamed on the Christians and Jews. Satan is the great liar and deceiver. If you are not rooted deep in your faith, if you are living a life of sin, then you will be the first to fall away and stop going to church.

Jesus said to be either hot or cold, be for me or against me. How will you stand for Christ during the persecution of the church if you will not let Christ into your life to cleanse you of all unrighteousness when the days are full of light and people prosper? Ye must walk in the light and repent of your sins.

"As for me and my house, we will serve the Lord. Amen" (Josh. 24:15).

The Hinge Pin

At the men's group meeting, I went up for prayer and I told the story of how my two sons had died and also their wives and my brother. Then my stepdaughter Jennifer died when she lost control of her motorcycle.

Dan, the guitar player, then told me that the Lord says there was a generational curse in the family. But because I have accepted and followed Jesus Christ the gates of hell that had been opened due to the generational curse have swung closed because of my commitment to Christ. And just like a hinge pin on a gate is under pressure, so has been my life. But I should rejoice because the next generation and generations to come will be blessed. The Bible says blessings to a thousand generations.

I do feel the pressure, and sometimes it overwhelms me, and I don't feel like fighting anymore. But I remember what God said to Paul, "My grace is sufficient for thee." So my prayer is this: "Lord, let thy will be done on earth, as it is in heaven. The Lord giveth and the Lord taketh away. Blessed be the Name of the Lord. But, please, Lord, no more children dying young. This is too much to bear. Amen."

The Rapture

"Behold I shew you a mystery; we shall not all sleep, but we shall all be changed. In a moment, in the twinkling of an eye, at the last trump: for the trumpet shall sound, and the dead shall be raised incorruptible, and we shall be changed. For this corruptible must put on incorruption, and this mortal must put on immortality" (1 Cor. 15:51–53).

"For the Lord himself shall descend from heaven with a shout, with the voice of the arch-angel, and with the trump of God: and the dead in Christ shall rise first. Then we which are alive and remain shall be caught up together with them in the clouds to meet the Lord in the air: and so shall we ever be with the Lord. Wherefore comfort one another with these words" (1 Thess. 4:16–18).

When you feel stressed and weary from the pressures of this life, cheer up. Someday we will be raptured, and we will leave all our troubles behind. Amen.

The Earthquake

There was an earthquake last night in Haiti. It measured 7.0 on the Richter Scale and devastated the capital of Port Au Prince. My heart goes out to the people of Haiti that lost loved ones and suffered in the destruction.

I looked in my Bible to get a word from the Lord. In Luke 13:1–5, Jesus spoke concerning the Galileans that were killed by

Pilate and had their blood mingled with their sacrifices and there were eighteen that were killed when the tower at Siloam fell on them. First they asked Jesus if this happened because they were worse sinners than the rest of the people, and Jesus's reply was, "I tell you, Nay; but except ye repent, ye shall all likewise perish."

Jesus then gives the parable of the fig tree that gave no fruit for three years and the master wanted to cut it down. The gardener asked to keep it for yet another year to see if it would bear fruit.

Jesus is patient with us, but he wants us to look within, judge ourselves, and repent. Sooner or later, our time will run out and we will face God's judgment. So it is better to repent sooner than later. When disaster strikes, are you prepared to meet the Lord?

Walking with God

The Christian walk is a daily walk. Each day is a gift from God. Each day is divided into day and night, and each day is divided into hours and minutes. It is by God's grace that we can experience His peace over a section of time without being interrupted by Satan.

In order to receive His grace, we must put on the mind of Christ. This is not possible if we are walking in the flesh with a carnal mind-set. So die to the flesh—that is, put your fleshly desires on the cross of Christ and die to the flesh, like Jesus died on the cross. Like Christ was raised up from the dead, we can be renewed in our mind and have victory over the flesh. Will we stumble and fall from grace? Yes! Do we accept defeat? No! Let us learn by our failures not to be defeated.

Therefore, we seek God's grace to carry us through the evil days, not to fail but to be victorious. We will then bask in the light of Christ and feel a new confidence in the grace of God! Amen.

Tithing 10 Percent?

"Will a man rob God? Yet ye have robbed me. But ye say, wherein have we robbed thee? In tithes and offerings" (Mal. 3:8).

There are blessings to those that pay God the tithe. When we give 10 percent of our income to our church, we have put our finances under God's blessings. He is faithful to provide us with all that we need as we pray for godly wisdom. God is so good to us. He only asks for 10 percent, and he leaves the other 90 percent for our earthly good use. We are also to give offerings as we see a need.

Does God need our money? Yes and no. Yes, if we are to build up God's kingdom on earth from our human understanding, it costs money to maintain a church building and pay the staff. No, not really because God is the owner of everything. Nothing was made without Jesus there to oversee it being made. Remember this, God doesn't live in a building. But when we have church services on Sunday, we expect God to show up! Don't put too much of your time and energy into talking about the tithe. If you are too focused on tithing as an act of performing a righteous duty to earn points with God for doing good works and thinking that you are better than other Christians, then you will become self-righteous and what was meant to be a blessing will become a thorn in your flesh. Remember that our salvation wasn't bought with money; it was paid for by the blood of Jesus Christ. So give generously what you can afford. You are not under the law but under grace. Don't act like the scribes and Pharisees.

> "Woe unto you, scribes and Pharisees, hypocrites! For ye devour widows' houses, and for a pretence make long prayer: therefore ye shall receive the greater damnation" (Matt 23:14).

One Way

> "Jesus saith unto him, I am the way, the truth and the life; no man cometh unto the Father, but by Me" (John 14:6).

There are many religions in the world and many different beliefs. The world will say there are many ways to get to heaven, but Jesus says there is only one way. Yes, one way to the Father, which is

God. And one way to Jesus, which is to be called by the Father. Jesus and the Father are One and the same. Or let me say, they are two in perfect agreement. Then when we add the Holy Spirit, we now have three together as one: the Trinity.

God wants us to be in agreement with Him. This is how we find Jesus and thus find God.

We need to study the Holy Bible (King James) to learn what manner of life we are to live. How can we live a life of sin and say we know God? How can we serve the devil and say we serve Jesus? Do not be blinded by the world and its lies and deception. If you don't have a personal relationship with Jesus Christ, then you are walking in darkness. If you say you have a personal relationship with Jesus and are living in sin daily, then you are still walking in darkness. It is time to step into the light of Jesus. Amen.

Keep the Sabbath Day

"Keep the Sabbath day to sanctify it, as the Lord thy God hath commanded thee. Six days shall thou labor, and do all thy work: But the seventh day is the Sabbath of the Lord thy God: in it thou shall not do any work, thou, nor thy son, nor thy daughter, nor thy manservant, not thy maidservant, nor thine ox, nor thy stranger, that is within thy gates; that thy manservant and thy maidservant may rest as well as thou. And remember that thou wast a servant in the land of Egypt, and that the Lord thy God brought thee out thence through a mighty hand and by a stretched out arm: therefore, the Lord thy God commanded thee to keep the Sabbath day" (Deut. 5:12–15).

It is very important to keep the Sabbath day. I understand that some people need to work on the Sabbath to keep their jobs, but it wasn't always like it is today. There is a difference between emergency work, necessity, and just plain greed for monetary gain. I pray God to give discernment, and may God's peace be with you. Amen.

Faith vs. Riches

> "Go to now, ye rich men, weep and howl for your miseries that shall come upon you" (James 4:1).
>
> "That the trial of your faith being much more precious than of gold that perisheth, though it be tried with fire, might be found unto praise and honor and glory at the appearing of Jesus Christ" (1 Pet. 1:7).

The world chases after money, riches, materialism. The Bible says that the rich men will weep and howl. When the markets crash and the banks fail, the rich men will watch as their god of money fails them.

Those that have invested into God's kingdom, however, by paying their tithes to the church and giving to the poor will have an eternal heavenly reward. Think of it as an investment. If you know how interest compounds over time, then you can appreciate the possibility of an eternal investment in heavenly places. How about an investment with no risk of ever losing the principle and one that will grow over the years and never lose a penny. Well, that is why I feel confident in investing my money into God's kingdom more than in this world's financial system.

> "Lay not up for yourselves treasures upon earth, where moth and rust doth corrupt, and where thieves break through and steal: But lay up for yourselves treasures in heaven, where neither moth nor rust doth corrupt, and where thieves do not break through nor steal: For where your treasure is, there will your heart be also" (Matt. 6:19, 20, 21).

What you do in your life on earth will reflect what rewards you will receive in heaven. Jesus talked about different crowns that can be earned, the soul winner's crown, the martyr's crown, etc. Jesus also mentioned that he was going to prepare a place for those that obey his commands and in His Father's house are many mansions.

Then the Bible talks about the wood, hay, and stubble being burned up, and only the things that are done for Christ and His kingdom will be able to withstand the fire of God's judgments. Things that cannot be seen by the world like faith, hope, mercy, love, long-suffering, chastity, pureness in heart, modesty, humility, and patience—these are more precious than gold and have eternal rewards.

There is no way to fool God, and you cannot buy with money the fruits of the Spirit. A modestly dressed woman that is pure in heart before God is more beautiful than the scantily dressed sex symbols that Hollywood produces. All the money in the world cannot buy a pure heart before God.

No wonder most rich people are going to weep and howl like dogs. It will be too late. Life will be over, and it will be time to stand before God.

Thank you for your Word, Lord Jesus. Amen.

Deadly Sin

> "If any man see his brother sin a sin which is not unto death, he shall ask, and he shall give him life for them that sin not unto death. There is a sin unto death: I do not say that he shall pray for it. All unrighteousness is sin, and there is a sin not unto death. We know that whosoever is born of God sinneth not; but he that is begotten of God keepeth himself, and that wicked one toucheth him not. And we know that we are of God, and the whole world lieth in wickedness" (1 John 5:16–19).

There are some sins that are deadly, and if you die while having a deadly sin in your soul, you will go to hell. It will not matter if you are born again and baptized or sing in the choir. It doesn't matter if you are a pastor, pope, or president. It does not matter if your pastor taught you once saved, always saved. I write this to warn you that there are certain deadly sins that you cannot keep on your favorite list and expect to gain entry into heaven. The Bible lists these sins in several places. If you are worried, then I suggest you read your Bible and find out what are these deadly sins.

Don't be ignorant to deadly sins that will send you to hell. I didn't know that witchcraft was a deadly sin until I read Galatians chapter 5:19,20,21:"Now the works of the flesh are manifest, which are these, adultery fornication, uncleanness, lasciviousness, idolatry, witchcraft, hatred, variance, emulations, wrath, strife, seditions, heresies, envyings, murders, drunkeness, revellings and such like: of the which I tell you before, as I also have told you in times past, that they that do such things shall not inherit the kingdom of God."

How much time are you investing in your eternal soul? Beware of the reaper; we don't know when he will come. Thank you, Jesus, for your Word. Amen.

The Great I AM

> "I Am the Lord thy God, which brought thee out of the land of Egypt, from the house of bondage. Thou shalt have none other gods before me. Thou shalt not make thee any graven image, or any likeness of anything that is in heaven above, or that is in the earth beneath, or that is in the waters beneath the earth; Thou shalt not bow down thyself unto them, nor serve them: for I the Lord thy God am a jealous God, visiting the iniquity of the fathers upon the children unto the third and fourth generation of them that hate me, and showing mercy unto thousands of them that love me and keep my commandments"(Deut. 5:6–10).

These five verses are just the first commandment. They say a lot more than what we were taught by the one liners of the Ten Commandment plaques they sell in the Christian bookstores.

Let's look at Deuteronomy 4:2: Ye shall not add unto the Word which I command you, neither shall ye diminish ought from it, that ye may keep the commandments of the Lord your God which I command you." Amen.

Take His Name

> "Thou shalt not take the name of the Lord thy God in vain: for the Lord will not hold him guiltless that taketh His name in vain" (Deut. 5:11).

One definition of the word *take* is to lay hold, to take root, or begin to grow; to unite successfully, to graft; to pick out, to select or choose.

The word *vain* means empty, devoid of real value, fruitless, utter ineffectiveness.

This commandment means much more than cursing God or swearing using His name. There are many people that call themselves Christians but are Christian in name only. Thus, they are guilty of taking the name of the Lord in vain. Wearing a cross as a piece of jewelry doesn't make a person closer to God either. Look at how some of the European explorers treated the Native Americans. Some professing to be Christians acted like the devil for the love of money. Also the slave traders and slave owners that claimed the name of Christ. I believe there will be former slaves in heaven looking down on former slave owners in hell.

Unless Jesus has taken root in your life and your life is bearing spiritual fruit, which should be apparent to those that know us, then you have taken the Lord's name in vain and you will not be guiltless on Judgment Day! Amen.

Honor

> "Honour thy father and thy mother as the Lord thy God has commanded thee; that thy days

may be prolonged, and that it may go well with thee, in the land which the Lord thy God giveth thee"(Deut. 5:16).

Lord, I thank you for my mother and father. I know they were not perfect in raising us children, but in order to be faithful to obeying this commandment, I must honor my parents for their self-sacrifice. Some have better parenting skills, while some parents are abusive and/or negligent in some areas. But as long as they remain in the home and try to raise their children, they deserve some respect. Raising children requires some degree of self-sacrifice, something that may not be appreciated until years later. As adult children we sometimes focus more on the bad times growing up. We should direct our thoughts to remember more of the good times. You will never know what it's like to raise children until you have children of your own.

Mother and Father, I thank you for being there for me. And for that I honor you both! Amen.

Murder

"Thou shalt not kill" (Deut. 5:17).

This commandment tells me how wrong abortion is. This is why I support the Right to Life organization. I believe that our nation is under a curse because as a nation, we have allowed over sixty million abortions. Let me say it another way: sixty million murders for nothing more than inconvenience or for lack of responsibility, or let's say, to cover up sin.

Are there exceptions to this commandment? Of course. God gave us a brain to reason. The mother's health, deformed baby, rape, incest, etc. I believe that some circumstances require the advice of the medical professionals. But let's face it, the majority of abortions do not fall into those categories. Most abortions are a means to erase the results of sexual sin or for the love of money. Raising children is expensive.

Now as to killing as a capital punishment, only for the worst crimes, but as to defend our country, yes. War is not pretty but necessary to hold back evil, the same as self-defense. It is a man's responsibility to defend and protect his home and family but only as a last resort should a person take a life. I pray I will never have to kill! Amen.

Adultery

> "Neither shall thou commit adultery" (Deut. 5:18).

Every act of adultery is preceded by a thought. First, the devil enters the mind. Once the devil plants a seed in our mind, it is up to us to remove that seed before it takes root. If we allow the seed to remain planted in our mind, it will grow to be a stronghold. Once the devil has built his stronghold, then the thoughts become acts. There is a fine line that separates thoughts from actions, the spirit world from the physical world, fantasy from reality. We are setting ourselves up to commit adultery.

Remember that the devil is a liar and the father of lies. That is why we must be careful what we see, hear, and think. The devil will try to convince us that we cannot sin in our mind. The devil will say a thought is not a sin until it is completed in the flesh. But Jesus said in Matthew 5:28, "But I say unto you, that whosoever looketh on a woman to lust after her hath committed adultery with her already in his heart."

> "For though we walk in the flesh, we do not war after the flesh: (For the weapons of our warfare are not carnal, but mighty through God to the pulling down of strongholds;) Casting down imaginations, and every high thing that exalteth itself against the knowledge of God, and bringing into captivity every thought to the obedience of Christ" (2 Cor. 10:3, 4, 5).

Stealing

"Neither shall thou steal" (Deut. 5:19).

Our God is our provider. He knows what we need, when we need it. What we need is not the same as what we want. The Bible also tells us to be content with what we have. The reason for that is so we don't become covetous, which may tempt us to steal.

"Let your conversation be without covetousness; and be content with such things as ye have: for he hath said, 'I will never leave thee, nor forsake the'" (Heb. 13:5).

Now there are different ways we can steal something: robbery, armed robbery, shoplifting, breaking and entering to burglarize. These are obvious crimes that face severe penalties.

Then there are other ways to steal that are harder to identify, such as tax evasion, white collar thefts, falsifying documents for gain, misrepresentation to clients, overcharging customers, laying claim to goods that don't belong to us.

Then there are thefts of a spiritual nature: robbing God by not supporting the church, taking the credit for another's achievements, stealing someone's joy by being negative and mean-spirited. Whatever the sin, it is time to repent and ask God's forgiveness. Be mature in Christ and walk in a worthy manner to His calling. Amen.

Thy Neighbor

"Neither shalt thou bear false witness against thy neighbor" (Deut. 5:20).

Jesus tells us to love our neighbor as ourselves and to do unto others as we would have them do unto us. I think it would be safe to say that the word *neighbor* could be inclusive of everyone that crosses our path in life. To bear false witness would be telling a lie about our neighbor. Sometimes gossiping may fall into that category. That is why it is wise to think before we speak and to choose our words carefully.

Thou Shalt Not Covet

> "Neither shalt thou desire thy neighbor's wife, neither shalt thou covet thy neighbor's house, his field, or his manservant or his maidservant, his ox, or his ass or anything that is thy neighbor's" (Deut. 5:21).

Desire means an expressed wish, a longing, craving.
Covet means to desire, to long for, to crave.
Content means having the desires limited to that which one has; satisfied.

Jesus said having food and shelter and clothing, be content with what you have.

The key to successful living is being content with what we have. God knows what we need and how much we can handle. Instead of looking at what others have, we need to focus on what God has given us and be thankful. To be covetous is to never be satisfied. It is important to establish healthy boundaries so we don't cross over the line and fall into sin.

Perfection vs. Holiness

Perfection is what we try for in the flesh but is not attainable by any human being. Holiness is from God and was made available only through Jesus Christ. There is an outward appearance that is man's attempt to perfect himself, and the end result is self-righteousness and failure. Then there is true holiness that is a manifestation of the Holy Spirit. True holiness is when the Christian matures to the place where the fruit of the Spirit is evident in that person's life. Holiness is not perfection because if we could reach a state of perfection, then we would no longer need God. Therefore, our imperfect sinfulness cries out to Jesus for forgiveness and produces a desire and a longing for the holiness of Christ. It is what we can experience from time to time as we strive for perfection. Holiness is felt when we have victory over sin and draw closer to God, either by reading the Bible or praise and worship, hearing anointed preaching, praying and fasting, or suffering persecution as Christians. Holiness can produce a peace in the midst of the many spiritual storms that rage around us. The flesh is always at war with the spirit, but when I put on the mind of Christ, then I become holy for that instant. Why? Because Jesus is the only perfect, Lamb of God. So perfect that to speak or read or think His Name, His Holiness can transcend to our spirit, our mind, and our body. Walk the narrow path with Jesus and experience a life of peace in a world gone mad. Amen.

> "But now being made free from sin, and become servants to God, ye have your fruit unto holiness, and the end everlasting life" (Rom. 6:22).
> "But the fruit of the Spirit is love, joy, peace, long-suffering, gentleness, goodness, faith, meekness, temperance: against such there is no law"(-Gal. 5:22).

The Spirit of Truth

> "Howbeit when he, the Spirit of Truth, is come, he will guide you into all truth: for he shall not speak of himself, but whatsoever he shall hear, that shall he speak: and he will shew you things to come" (John 16:13).

It is important for Christians to speak the truth in love, not to condemn the sinner but to help them to find the narrow path. It is not easy, but it is necessary.

When Christians gather together to have fellowship, it can be a fun and uplifting time. There is, however, a serious aspect when the

Spirit of Truth shows up. Why? Because some people cannot handle the truth. Because some Christians are living openly in sin and are looking for acceptance from the body of Christ. The church no longer preaches repentance as a necessary step for salvation, thus weakening her stand against sin. As a result, evil creeps into the body of Christ like a virus that can weaken the whole body. May the Spirit of Truth guide us in every area of our lives. Amen.

> "And ye shall know the truth, and the truth shall make you free" (John 8:32).
> "Jesus saith unto him, "I am the way, the truth, and the life: no man cometh unto the Father, but by me" (John 14:6).

What Did Jesus Say?

> "And behold, one came and said unto him, Good Master, what good thing shall I do that I may have eternal life. And he said unto him, 'Why callest thou me good? There is none good but one, that is God: but if thou wilt enter into life, keep the commandments.' He saith unto him, which? Jesus said, 'Thou shalt do no murder, thou shalt not commit adultery, thou shalt not steal, thou shalt not bear false witness, Honor thy father and thy mother: and thou shalt love thy neighbor as thyself'" (Matt. 19:16–19).

Now this is what Jesus said was necessary to have eternal life. Obey the commandments of God. When we try and fail, we have an advocate to bridge the gap to the Father in Jesus Christ. Jesus didn't come to do away with the law; Jesus came to fulfill the law. The Ten Commandments are just as relevant today as when they were written by the finger of God and given to Moses thousands of years ago.

Jesus Christ is our foundation. Jesus told Peter, "Upon this rock will I build my kingdom." A kingdom or castle is comprised of many stones that have to be cut and fitted. Ten of these stones are in the foundation wall. On these ten stones are the Ten Commandments. For anyone to dismiss them as not being relevant to Christianity today is blinded to God's truth and God's character. Help us, Lord, to see! Amen. Malachi 3:6 says, "For I am the Lord, I change not."

Why Choose the King James Version

> "But I say unto you, that whosoever is angry with his brother without a cause shall be in danger of the judgment" (Matt. 5:22, KJV).
>
> "But I tell you that anyone who is angry with his brother will be subject to judgment". (Matt. 5:22, NIV).

The people that wrote the NIV Bible and the other translations have changed the wording in many verses. And by changing the wording, they change the meaning. The implications to the above verse are staggering, and this is just one example. God made man in His image. We get angry just like God gets angry, but as Christians, we need to discern between evil anger and righteous anger. An example of righteous anger could be a reaction to Hollywood spewing out films filled with adultery, sexuality, murder, witchcraft, violence, rape, etc.

If you believed the NIV verse to mean you should never get angry, then someone has been successful in silencing Christians. If Satan's goal is to burn all Bibles and silence Christians, then he is off to a good start, burning the King James Bible one word at a time. God, show us your pure meaning in all scripture. Amen.

Many Deceivers

> "For many shall come in My name saying, I am Christ; and shall deceive many" (Matt. 24:5).

This is one sign that the end is near. I have heard of a few men in the world that call themselves Jesus Christ, and they are quite delusional. What Jesus is referring to in that verse, however, has a deeper meaning; rather, anyone that seems to have a different image of who Jesus Christ really is and comes preaching a different gospel that is contrary to what Jesus taught us in His word.

Let's face it there are so many different religions within Christianity today. It seems that within each religion are men and women that have differing opinions as to who Jesus was or what Jesus taught. Where is the unity and agreement within the body of Christ? Who will be saved? Everyone that can blurt out the name of Christ at the last trumpet call regardless of their life's sinfulness? No, I think not. Jesus taught repentance and obedience to the commandments of God as the way to eternal life. So do not be deceived by smooth talkers. There is only one narrow path! And the only thing that will keep you from finding that narrow path is Satan blocking your way. If there are one hundred different opinions as to the meaning and message of the gospel of Christ, then according to Galatians 1:8 and 1:9, then the ninety-nine are accursed and only one is the true gospel of Christ.

> "But though we or, an angel from heaven, preach any other gospel unto you than that which we have preached unto you, let him be accursed. As we said before, so say I now again, if any man preach any other gospel unto you than that which we have preached unto you, let him be accursed" (Gal. 1:8,9).

Rebellion and Witchcraft

> "For rebellion is as the sin of witchcraft, and stubbornness is as iniquity and idolatry. Because thou hast rejected the Word of the Lord, he hath also rejected thee from being king" (1 Sam. 15:23).

Rebellion against God is refusing to be obedient to His commandments. Saul rebelled by not destroying all that God commanded by the prophet Samuel. Saul and the people were obedient to God but not 100 percent. Does that describe the church today?

Why is rebellion like witchcraft? Rebellion against God is man telling God, "I know more than God and therefore I will be my own god." Witchcraft may or may not acknowledge God as God, but the witch claims to be able to make things happen by their own doings, such as casting spells, making potions, having special charms, amulets, and all manner of abominations. The reason these witches have supernatural power is because they are channeling the powers of hell. And that is where they are destined to go when they die. The children are being encouraged to read books and watch movies that elevate the role models of witches and wizards. But what does the word of God say about these things?

Parents, if you care for your children, you must warn them! Parents, you must educate yourselves about the demonic influence that this has on you, your child, and your home. If God calls this an abomination, why would you allow Satan to tempt your child?

> "My people are destroyed for lack of knowlege: because thou hast rejected knowlege, I will also reject thee that thou shalt be no priest to me: seeing thou hast forgotten the law of thy God, I will also forget thy children" (Hos. 4:6).

If God commands that you shall not commit adultery and you do, then you are living in rebellion against God. It doesn't matter if you go to church and pay your tithes or sing in the choir or even if you are the pastor of the church. You are in rebellion against God, and if you don't repent and stop this rebellion, you will end up in hell. Hell has many rebels and witches. If you are a witch and you call yourself a good witch, you need to realize there is no such thing. All forms of witchcraft are from hell. The good news is Jesus will forgive you and restore you, but you need to repent of your sin and renounce all forms of witchcraft. This is necessary also for people that are fortune tellers, psychic, or those that claim to channel the dead. What they channel are demons, and they lead many to the path to hell.

Why do we rebel against God? Because of our stubbornness, which is as iniquity, and idolatry and iniquity is wickedness. And rebellion is like witchcraft.

Don't be deceived! You cannot fashion for yourselves a god that is customized for your own wants and needs. You may as well buy a statue and place it on a pedestal in your home and call that thing your god. Stubbornness is idolatry.

Repent and turn from your wicked ways! God will meet you where you are, no matter how deep you are in sin. If you feel you have been victorious over sin except for one area or one stronghold, then Satan has power over your will. God wants you 100 percent, not because He needs you but because you need Him. Without God, you face death and hell. There are no other options. Life or death; heaven or hell. Are you obedient or rebellious? The choice is yours. Step up by faith.

The Great Persecution

> "Now the brother shall betray the brother to death, and the father the son; and children shall rise up against their parents, and shall cause them to be put to death" (Mark 13:12).
>
> "And ye shall be betrayed both by parents and brethren, and kinsfolk and friends; and some of you shall they cause to be put to death" (Luke 21:16).

Something is going to happen; a big lie and a great deception will be perpetuated. A great delusion will be taught worldwide. This could be a declassified document or secret or a new discovery found on earth or from outer space. It may be linked to UFOs or have something to do with alien life-forms. Whatever it is, it is evil. No matter what the news reports or what the scientists say, it is going to be a big lie.

The end result of the big lie will be to disprove the existence of God. The schools will be required to teach that God doesn't exist, and the laws will turn against Christianity. They will teach that man is his own god and will require everyone to worship an image. People will fall into a state of moral depravity. The schools will give new meaning to sex education. Anything and everything will be taught as normal. Parents and churches that take a stand against this immorality will be ridiculed and penalized. There will be fines and legal action taken against the godly and outspoken:

many churches will close, Christians will have to meet in secret in homes, home Bible studies will be outlawed, neighbor will turn in neighbor for holding prayer group meetings in their homes. Eventually, Christians will be outlaws and have a bounty paid to the person that turns them in.

The prison camps will be overcrowded, and then the executions will begin. The guillotine will be used to behead the Christians. The news people will spread the lies that the Christians are to blame for all the world's problems and so they must be exterminated.

The Beast, 666, the Antichrist will have a huge image created and command everyone to worship his image. Everyone will have to receive a mark on their hand or forehead in order for them to be able to buy or sell. Anyone who refuses to take this mark will be put to death.

My advice is to pray and purify your soul by the blood of Christ before the insanity begins.

To be free of sin is to be free indeed. God will have mercy to those that earnestly seek Him. Don't put it off; tomorrow is not guaranteed. Amen.

God's Grace

> "For by grace are ye saved through faith, and that not of yourselves; it is the gift of God. Not of works lest any man should boast" (Eph. 2:8, 9).

This explains that we are saved by God's grace, but that saving grace is our escape from the fires of hell. If after we are saved we run back into the fire, then whose fault is it when we burn?

> "Certain men, ungodly men, turning the grace of our God into lasciviousness, denying God and Jesus Christ" (Jude 4)
> "By whom we have received grace and apostleship, for obedience to the faith" (Rom. 1:5).
> "Even so faith, if it hath not works, is dead, being alone" (James 2:17).

Some people preach that our salvation is all God's grace and nothing that we do, not our works, etc. This is wrong teaching. You have to look at being saved by grace as a progression of events. First, God's grace calls us out of darkness, then our faith is activated to move in the right direction. We then are taught by the Bible how to live our lives. We get delivered from all our uncleanness by repenting and asking God to forgive us because we are truly sorry for sinning. Then by faith, we move into working out our salvation. Then doing the works of God, such as spreading the good news of the gospel to the lost around the world. We need to read the whole Bible, for it is all good! Amen.

> "Wherefore, my beloved, as ye have always obeyed, not as in my presence only, but now much more in my absence, work out your own salvation with fear and trembling"(Phil. 2:12).
> "My grace is sufficient for thee: for my strength is made perfect in weakness" (2 Cor. 12:9).

Did you ever have a habit or addiction or a sin that had a grip on your life? You prayed for deliverance from it to no avail, only to feel like, *This is just going to be with me until I die.* Then when we feel like giving up, we are touched by God's grace and we receive an answer to our prayers. Amen.

In my weakness, I felt God's grace come over me. I sought God by reading His word and praying all the more. It is experiences like this that make God's grace real and not just a word. This grace can also be described as a helper of pure love and holiness that can transform a sinner into a saint. Not for us to take credit for our accomplishments, by saying I did this and I did that, no, but rather to give our Lord Jesus Christ the glory for elevating us out of the pit of despair by His grace. Thank you, Jesus, for being real in my life! Amen.

What Would Jesus Say?

> "And he said unto them, go ye into all the world, and preach the gospel to every creature. He that believeth and is baptized shall be saved, but he that believeth not shall be damned."(Mark 16:15, 16).

There was a new fad someone started called WWJD (What would Jesus do?) T-shirts, bracelets, etc. bore these initials. It is good to do good works of love and reach out to the lost. We must never forget the great commission of Jesus to His disciples. The contrast of such love is the ultimate in punishment for those that reject Jesus Christ. Some things that Jesus said are so powerful and strong that most Christians today try to avoid speaking or quoting Jesus due to the fact that they don't want to face Jesus's true nature or they are afraid they will offend someone. Some people try to put Christ in this little box that they carry in their pocket. And when the Holy Spirit convicts them of their sins, they take out that little box and say, "My Jesus has already forgiven me of my sins," without any notion of repenting from that sin. They want their sins to be accepted by Jesus, or they will come up with ideas like God is love, therefore he would never do anything to hurt us no matter what we do in life! Well, the truth is, the Bible describes a place called hell where people are in torment day and night for eternity! Why? Because not only do they love the sin, they teach it to others as something to be desired as normal behavior. Pray, pray, pray, always! Amen.

Mercy

"Blessed are the merciful; for they shall obtain mercy" (Matt. 5:7).

"And he said, He that shewed mercy on him. Then said Jesus unto him, go and do thou likewise" (Luke 10:37).

Dictionary - Mercy = Compassionate treatment of an offender or adversary.

No one is perfect; we all need God's mercy when it comes to being judged for our sins. So God, by His mercy, can show us compassion in His judgments.

Another type of mercy is in helping people that we don't like or people that are far away, suffering some misfortune or natural disaster. We can read about their devastation while eating breakfast and listening to the morning news and not miss a spoonful of cereal.

Jesus Christ is a stumbling block and offensive to those in the world that are lost or reject Him. Christians, however, are always the first in line to volunteer to help people around the world. That is God's mercy displayed through people, and that is a good example of the compassion of Jesus Christ. Lord, have mercy! Amen.

A Hedge of Protection

"Hast not thou made an hedge about him, and about his house, and about all that he hath on every side? Thou hast blessed the work of his hands, and his substance is increased in the land" (Job 1:10). Lord, I pray a hedge of protection around myself, my family, my possessions; and I also pray for a blessing on my finances. Amen.

There is a spiritual hedge that cannot be penetrated by Satan. Some say that once that hedge is in place, the only way Satan can enter into the life of a born-again Christian is through the front door and he (Satan) has to ask for our permission to enter.

Have you ever had to deal with a high-pressure salesman at your door? I have in the past, and once you let him in, he is very hard to get rid of. Well, imagine how much harder it is to get Satan out of your house after you let him in.

The best thing to do is to not answer the door when Satan comes knocking. Beware of Satan when he disguises himself to gain access to your home, your family, your heart and mind. Satan and his demons can enter your home by attaching themselves to certain objects that you allow to be brought into the home. These are evil objects that give the demons a legal right to enter and build a stronghold. As an example, you may pray for godly protection over your house and then bring in a Ouija board or tarot cards. Not too smart, you have just allowed the devil access. That is why it is so important to know the difference between good and evil. The best defensive move is the move of the Holy Spirit. Seek the Holy Spirit daily, and you will be sensitive to any evil that may be in your home. If I feel an evil presence, I will pray for divine protection in the name of Jesus Christ. Sometimes it may be necessary to do a house clearing/cleaning. After that go from room to room with anointing oil and take authority over each room and command the demons to leave in the name of Jesus. Don't be afraid and do not doubt the power of Christ. And they must leave because they no longer have permission or legal authority to reside there. Lord Jesus, thank you for your hedge of protection. Amen.

The Jewish People

"Jerusalem, Jerusalem, thou that killest the prophets, and stonest them which are sent unto thee, how often would I have gathered thy children together, even as a hen gathers her chickens under her wings, and ye would not! Behold, your house is left unto you desolate. For I say unto you, ye shall not see me henceforth, till ye say, 'Blessed is he that cometh in the name of the Lord'" (Matt. 23:37–39).

Jesus is a Jew, a direct descendant of King David, on his mother's side; but his father is God the Father. The Jews didn't accept Jesus as their messiah because they didn't want to walk the narrow path that Jesus talked about. The Jewish leaders wanted to remain in power, and they saw Jesus as a threat to their position of power over the people. That is why they called for Jesus to be crucified. It wasn't Pontius Pilate that called for Jesus to be crucified.

> "When Pilate saw that he could prevail nothing, but that rather a tumult was made, he took water, and washed his hands before the multitude, saying, I am innocent of the blood of this just person: see ye to it" (Matt. 27:24, 25).

The Jews have been persecuted many times throughout history. Their prayers were not heard because they didn't pray to God the Father in the name of his only begotten Son, Jesus Christ, the Messiah. I don't mean to sound cruel, but this is true. Jesus said you can't get to the Father without going through him. I didn't say it; Jesus said it. The Jews also spoke a curse on themselves.

> "Then answered all the people, and said, His blood be on us and our children" (Matt. 27:26).

My message to the Jewish people is, it's okay to believe in Jesus. He won't hurt you. Jesus loves you more than you can imagine. You are His people, He died for you. All you have to do is open the door to your heart and invite Him in. There is a special symbol worn around the neck or as a pin on the person who is a Jew and has accepted Jesus as Lord. It is the Star of David with a cross in the middle. The book of Revelation predicts that during the seven-year tribulation God is going to select 12,000 Jewish Christians from each of the twelve tribes of Israel, for a total of 144,000 men, that will receive a seal of divine protection from the Antichrist. They will have power from God to preach the Gospel around the world and will evangelize and lead many Jews to Jesus Christ.

I challenge all Jews to read the New Testament and pray for God to speak to you. Your life will never be the same. You will have a double blessing. You can still keep your Jewish heritage and be filled with the Holy Spirit and walk in the light, love, and power of Jesus Christ. You will need Jesus in these last days before He returns, more than ever! It is prophesied that in the last days Israel will be attacked from the north. It is also prophesied that most Jews will be fooled by the Antichrist in the last seven years before Jesus returns. You will know you have been fooled by the false messiah when he sits in the temple and proclaims to be God and he defiles the temple in Jerusalem. It is described in Daniel and Matthew 24 as the abomination of desolation. Seek Jesus while you can. Time is running out! Amen.

Law and Grace

> "Even when we were dead in sins, hath he quickened us together with Christ (by grace are ye saved)" (Eph. 2:5).
> "For by grace are ye saved through faith; and that not of yourselves, it is the gift of God" (Eph. 2:8).

It is by God's grace that you could say we have been called to serve in God's army. We had faith that was activated by grace. Now, once we said the sinner's prayer, that was like being sworn into the military service. Now that we are serving in God's army, it is important to know that, even in the army, there is a military code of conduct that we must live by or be punished. That is where the law comes in to play. It is God's laws and commandments that help keep us on that narrow path. That is to say, the law shows us when we stray from the narrow path. Once we are saved, we are subject to godly discipline as sons and daughters of God.

To Other World Religions

> "Verily I say unto you, whosoever shall not
> receive the kingdom of God as a little child shall
> in no wise enter therein" (Luke 18:17)
> "Woe unto you, when all men shall speak
> well of you! For so did their fathers to the false
> prophets" (Luke 6:26, 27).

But I say unto you that hear, love your enemies. Do good to them that hate you. You cannot fight evil with evil. Turn to Jesus and learn the ways of love. Don't be fooled by the lies of Satan. You can only get to heaven by going through the gate. Jesus Christ is the gate, the only gate.

The Bible is the only written Word of God that has been given to man. All other books are from man. Jesus Christ is not a prophet; all the prophets are dead. He is the one and only begotten Son of the one and only Living God. Jesus was crucified, and He died and was buried. On the third day he rose up from the dead and was seen by over five hundred people. He then rose up in the sky before their very eyes, up, up, and away, up to heaven and is seated at the right hand of God.

> "Neither is there salvation in any other: for there
> is none other name under heaven given among
> men, whereby we must be saved" (Acts 4:12).

Jesus will come again to gather his followers to life everlasting. He will also judge the world for its sin, and all who rejected him will be cast into hell for eternity. All false prophets, false religions, the devil and his demons shall be cast into the lake of fire with no way to escape. After this, the Lord will create a new earth where there will be no violence. The lion will lay down next to the lamb and will eat straw. A child will be able to pick up snakes and not be harmed. There will be a time of peace for one thousand years, then Satan will be let loose for a short time of testing, then he will be destroyed forever. You can be a part of this wonderful time of peace. All you have to do is make Jesus Lord of your life and obey His commandments. I pray for eyes to be opened in Jesus's Name. Amen.

Law and Grace

> "Think not that I am come to destroy the law or the prophets: I am not come to destroy, but to fulfill" (Matt. 5:17).

If we are called by God into His kingdom, by His grace are we saved and not by our works. That initial saving grace is the calling out of the world of sin to enter the kingdom of God.

Just like the induction into the army during a war, the army was not very strict as to its standards. All they were concerned with was getting lots of men together to fight in the war. As a matter of fact, if you looked at the guys getting off the bus at Fort Dix, New Jersey, you would say, they sure don't look like soldiers. Well, guess what? They were soldiers because they were all sworn in at the induction center but that was just the beginning of months of training. One of our many training classes was on the Military Code of Conduct. We were told that if we broke military laws or civilian laws, we would be punished.

The same is true in God's kingdom. If we break the Kingdom's laws, we will be punished by God. If we break the civil laws, we will be punished by man, sometimes by both God and man.

The Law Protects

God's commandments were given to us, not as a list of do's and don'ts by a mean Father but as a guideline to protect us, His children, from the evil consequences of sin.

> "The law of thy mouth is better unto me than thousands of gold and silver" (Ps. 119:72).

Lord, help us obey Your commandments. Amen.

"Verily, verily, I say unto you, the servant is not greater than his Lord; neither he that is sent greater than he that sent him" (John 13:16).

First of all, let me say that all the Bible is God-inspired and good for instruction, but when I am not sure of something that I read in the Old Testament or the other books in the New Testament, I go straight to the source.

I ask myself, "What did Jesus say?" So I go to the four gospels (Matthew, Mark, Luke, and John) and the Revelation. I feel comfort in reading what Jesus said. I feel comfort because I know that there is no greater authority in the universe than Jesus Christ.

What I write today is God-inspired. My motives are pure; I have no hidden agenda. I write to help someone in the future generations. I want to leave something of spiritual value when I am dead and gone home to heaven, but I am only human, and what I write is only God-inspired. To get the pure word is to read what Jesus said with confidence that every word is pure gold. Don't let fast talkers steer you in a different direction. Beware of wolves in sheep's clothing. Thank you, Jesus, for your Word! Amen.

The Gift of Heaven

"And that repentance and remission of sins should be preached in His name among all nations, beginning at Jerusalem" (Luke 24:47).

"For he is not a God of the dead, but of the living, for all live unto Him" (Luke 20:38).

"But they which shall be accounted worthy to obtain that world, and the resurrection from the dead, neither marry; nor are given in marriage. Neither can they die anymore: for they are equal to the angels; and are the children of God, being children of the resurrection" (Luke 20:35, 36).

It is so awesome and so hard to comprehend the free gift of salvation that Jesus had opened the door for mankind to be saved. The more I think about it, the more I am totally amazed at the gift of salvation: that Jesus, being perfect in every way, who never sinned, gave his life for me and you so we could be forgiven and be saved. I have heard the gospel message thousands of times, but now it has taken on a new importance in my life. Before me I see an open door and stairs leading up to heaven and a voice saying, "Come up here, my son, your sins have been forgiven, enter into everlasting life."

How can the world overlook such a wonderful thing? Jesus is so holy and so powerful that no man or woman could stand before Him without falling down on their knees. If Jesus allowed His full glory to shine, it would be so powerful that we would faint.

You and I are without excuse. There is no reason why any Christian should continue to live a life of sin after acknowledging Christ crucified for us. Do you understand the concept? There is no other sacrifice that will be accepted. Only Christ crucified can save us. Do you think that He gave His life so that we can continue to live in sin? No way! He died to save us from the sin life. When you grasp a hold of that concept, then and only then will your eyes be opened to walk the narrow path that Christ puts before you! Amen.

Fruit of the Spirit

> "But the fruit of the Spirit is love, joy, peace, long-suffering, gentleness, goodness, faith, meekness, temperance; against such, there is no law" (Gal. 5:22, 23).
>
> "Ye shall know them by their fruits. Do men gather grapes of thorns or figs of thistles? Even so, every good tree bringeth forth good fruit; but a corrupt tree bringeth forth evil fruit" (Matt. 7:16, 17).

Did you ever meet someone that had a peaceful spirit? I did. That person was my mother, Grace. I very seldom ever saw her get angry, and along with peace were all the other fruits also present in her life. Now these fruits were there. She was not a baby Christian trying to develop these fruits. As a matter of fact, she didn't read the Bible very often. She must have been born that way. I can't say enough good things about my mother.

I remember witnessing to my mother about how she needed to be born again and receive Jesus the way they teach it in the Pentecostal church. What I didn't realize at that time was that it was I who needed these fruits of the Spirit developed in my life. I needed to preach to myself. Amen.

Who Is a Christian?

> "And they overcame him (Satan) by the blood of
> the Lamb, and by the word of their testimony;
> and they loved not their lives unto the death"
> (Rev. 12:11).

If (when) the government outlaws Christianity and the police investigated you to see if they should place you under arrest, would they be able to find enough evidence to charge you?

Here is a list of some incriminating evidence the New World Order would look for:

1. Membership in a Christian church
2. Regular attendance
3. Involvement in ministries
4. Record of baptism
5. Faithful in tithes and offerings
6. What your neighbors say about you
7. What your family and friends would report about you
8. How many Bibles and Christian books are in your home
9. What is on your hard drive on your computer
10. Are you pro-life?

If there was enough evidence to prove you are a Christian, then rejoice! That means you may be counted worthy to suffer some persecution for your faith in Jesus. And great is your reward in heaven. But if they can't find enough evidence to charge you for being a Christian, then it's a time to mourn because you are a perfect candidate to receive the mark of the beast 666. Welcome to the NWO and prepare to drink of the wine of the wrath of God.

If you want to be counted as a Christian, then stop hiding and stand up and be counted as one worthy of the calling. Amen.

Sins of Omission

> "Verily, verily, I say unto thee, except a man be born again, he cannot see the Kingdom of God" (John 3:3).

The biggest sin anyone can commit is not acknowledging that they are a sinner in need of a Savior and that they need to be born again.

Being born again is real. If your life is not transformed, then you have not been born again. So go back to square one and start over; you missed the boat.

Are you giving to different missions to spread the gospel to a lost world? What about those that are starving or don't have access to clean drinking water. How about providing for your family? The Bible says that whoever doesn't provide for his/her own family is worse than an unbeliever. Would you rather spend your money on alcohol and/or drugs instead of putting food on the table? Love thy neighbor; love thine enemies; love thy family, church, country, minister; care for the sick. Did you ever empty a bedpan, change bedding, do laundry, bandage a wound, drive someone to church, doctor, dentist, hospital? Have you cried with someone at a funeral or visited the sick, the prisoner, the drug addict? Have you taught a child, played a game, gave a toy at Christmas? Smile at a stranger, paint a picture, go for a walk, be at peace with yourself and God. Forgive others, forgive yourself. Pray for peace. Amen.

Do Not Hoard

> "How hardly shall they that have riches enter
> into the Kingdom of God!" (Mark 10:23).

Now here is a man that has kept all the commandments since his youth. Jesus loved him and told him he needed to sell his possessions and give to the poor and follow Him, but the man was grieved and went away sad because he had many possessions. He was rich!

That is why I pray for God's provision, but only enough to be content. I have heard of rich people that were unhappy and some commit suicide. Some people like to hoard money. I once knew a man that talked about his money all the time, and some of the richest people are the stingiest people when it comes to giving to charity. As Christians we need to own our possessions and not let our possessions own us. Money is only a tool in my toolbox. No more important than my hammer or my saw. My source of provision for all my needs is my God. He shall provide me with whatsoever I need in this life. All I have to do is trust God and be content with what He has provided. Sometimes I want more; but I don't want to covet what I see that the world, the flesh, and the devil has to offer. The love of money is the root of evil.

> "For what does it profit a man, to gain the whole
> world and forfeit his life?"(Mark 8:36).
> "There is a way that seemeth right unto
> a man; but the end thereof are the ways of
> death."(Prov. 14:12).

The Bible says we should give, not to store up goods for ourselves. There was another man that had so much he wanted his servants to build new barns. Let's read what God said to that man in Luke12: 19, 20: "And I will say to my soul; Soul, thou hast much goods laid up for many years; take thine ease, eat, drink, and be merry. But God said unto him, Thou fool, this night thy soul shall be required of thee: then whose shall those things be, that thou hast provided?"

We need to use wisdom and have a healthy balance with our finances. We need to give generously at the proper time to where God wants us to give, and with a cheerful heart we give, not because someone pressures us to give as a requirement to earn points with God. We also need to remember that charity should begin at home. It's wrong to give so much to church that you can't afford to buy your children a pair of shoes. God is not a cruel tax collector. He loves you and your children, and God knows and understands our needs.

God's Spirit

"God is a Spirit: and they that worship Him must worship Him in spirit and in truth" (John 4:24).

To have a close spiritual worship experience with God, we need to prepare our spirit. We must find our spiritual self and purge all negative thoughts. Once the negativity is absent from our spirit, then we need to focus on everything that is holy, everything that is pure, everything that is lovely.

Remember that God is in a steady state of being. That is to say, He never changes in Spirit. This is important to know if we are going to be successful in our attempt to worship God. It says in Malachi 3:6, "For I am the Lord, I change not."

If you are having a hard time feeling close to God when you pray, in church, in worship, or if God seems far away, then it is time to examine your spirit with truth. When we purge evil from our spirit, then we feel closer to God's Spirit. God's spirit is always near. It is our sin that make us feel that God is far away. That is why we should not go by our feelings but to trust God. Sometimes many sins have to be removed before we can feel the holiness of God, and that is just a foretaste of greater things to come.

What Offends You?

> "The Son of Man shall send forth His angels, and they shall gather out of His kingdom all things that offend, and them which do iniquity; And shall cast them into a furnace of fire: there shall be wailing and gnashing of teeth. Then shall the righteous shine forth as the sun in the kingdom of their Father. Who hath ears to hear, let him hear" (Matt. 13:41–43).

Over the past twenty years, I have found that the more I read God's Word, the more sensitive my spirit became to the evil that has permeated our society. For example, I purchased a movie that I remembered from thirty years ago. I could remember that we all enjoyed it at the time, so I bought the DVD and put it on to watch at home that night. After the first few minutes into the movie, I had to tell the grandchildren to go to their rooms as there was cursing I didn't want them to hear. I was shocked at the cursing, the swearing, the sex, the drug use. The whole movie was very offensive to me. I was so upset that I broke it in half and threw it in the trash. What I learned by that experience was this: the more you follow the world and the more you expose your spirit to the evil of the world, your spirit will become so desensitized to evil that you will no longer be offended by it. That is what is happening to our society. The Internet has opened a Pandora's box of evil. If something is not done soon, we could see a new generation of totally desensitized people and a reemergence of Sodom and Gomorrah. If you are offended by evil, that is a good thing. You haven't been desensitized yet. But if you are offended by the Bible and preachers of righteousness, that is a bad sign. Your soul is in deep trouble. God's goodness never changes; we are the ones that change. We can change for good, or we can change for evil. When the people change for evil, then society is caught in a downward spiral and will eventually crumble from decay and corruption. But when the people change for the good as a direct result of the people repenting of their sins, then crime rate will be lowered and the people will prosper. Always try to seek after the good and let evil be offensive to your spirit. Read your Bible. There is power in God's Word.

Faith in Action

In the book of Luke 8:19, 20, Jesus's mother and brothers were trying to see Jesus, but the crowd prevented them from getting close. So someone told Jesus that his mother and brothers were in the crowd. Then Jesus gave this reply in verse 21. "My mother and brother are these which hear the Word of God and do it." In Matthew 12:49, "And he stretched forth his hand toward his disciples, and said, 'Behold my mother and my brethren.'"

Jesus said many things that have such a profound meaning. Throughout His three years of active ministry, Jesus had to deal with many people that were lacking in faith. He was also constantly trying to persuade the masses to repent and seek the kingdom of God that he was frustrated by their lack of faith. The above Bible verses show an emotional display of how much importance Jesus places on his disciples' faith and obedience. He also shows us that He does not give special treatment to anyone due to their social status or relation to his earthly family. This speaks volumes to Jesus being a fair and impartial judge and to the seriousness of His requirements to enter his kingdom.

> "And Jesus said unto him, 'Verily I say unto thee, Today shalt thou be with me in paradise'" (Luke 23:43)

I have heard many people quote the above Bible verse as a way for them to justify just how easy it is to gain entrance to heaven. I think that is so wrong to do so because of the unique circumstance of that particular situation. First of all, you and I are not nailed to a cross next to Jesus Christ. Secondly, the thief on the cross didn't have time to get baptized and study Jesus's teachings (we do). Thirdly, there were no Christian churches at that time. Fourth, even though the thief on the cross didn't even know who Jesus was, he admitted his own guilt and recognized Jesus as being innocent of any crime. Fifth, he asked Jesus to remember him when Jesus entered His kingdom, which showed that Jesus's divine nature was revealed to him. Therefore, when we read about the great faith that was displayed as faith in action by a man that couldn't even move, let's be humbled and get motivated to do even more for the kingdom of God, with the vast abundance of resources that God has blessed us with. Let this be a call to action, faith in action. Amen.

Don't Look Back

> "No man having put his hand to the plough and looking back, is fit for the kingdom of heaven" (Luke 9:62).

Jesus gave many examples of things that we need to act on to prove our faith. Why? So that when He returns in judgment, He will find us worthy to enter into His kingdom. Are we saved by God's grace or by our works? I say by a combination of both. First, by God's grace and the shed blood of Jesus on the cross. This is what opened the door, giving access heaven to all that truly believe in Jesus and forgiveness of sin. But to those that get lazy and fall into diverse temptations, using the grace of God as a license to continue living in sin, I say, woe unto you! For when Jesus returns, what will you say in your defense? But to those that are active in the faith and obey God's commandments, Jesus will say, "Well done, good and faithful servant. Enter into My kingdom, where I have prepared a place for you."

Love and Mercy

> "Love worketh no ill to his neighbor, therefore, love is the fulfilling of the law" (Rom. 13:10).
> "Hatred stirreth up strifes, but love covereth all sins." (Prov. 10:12).

> "Let us therefore come boldly unto the throne of grace, that we may obtain mercy, and find grace to help in time of need" (Heb. 4:16).

Isn't God wonderful! He knows the hardships we face every day, and He also knows our weaknesses and our heart. Let's face it, we have all done things in life that we regret. If God can forgive us our sins, then we need to forgive our brothers and sisters when they slip up.

But after love and mercy, the Bible says in Hebrews 4:16 that mercy comes from grace to help us in our times of need. Now we can use God's grace to gently guide others back to the narrow path of Christ. These three—love, mercy, and grace—are working together for a purpose. The purpose is to overcome sin, not to allow sin. When an infant falls down, we help them get up. When an adult falls down, we lovingly help them up and with mercy we point out what caused them to fall. Amen.

666 = WWW

> "And He causeth all, both small and great, rich and poor, free and bond, to receive a mark in their right hand, or in their foreheads; And that no man might buy or sell, save he that had the mark, or the name of the beast, or the number of his name. Here is wisdom. Let him that hath understanding count the number of the beast: for it is the number of a man; and his number is Six Hundred Three Score and Six" (Rev. 13:16–18).

With my right hand, I navigated the World Wide Web, controlling the mouse that was in my right hand. Then I entered my PIN number to access my bank account, which I memorized. You see, this takes place in the future, when the world's oil reserves are exhausted and personal transportation is outlawed. The New World Order has rationed all oil and gas reserves. Martial law has been declared, and people are forced to buy and sell through the internet.

All food and clothing has to be ordered online and delivered by government couriers or drones. The computers will all be tied together for security purposes, due to increased terrorist attacks around the world. Some Christians have moved to secret locations and are bartering their goods and services in order to exist. Pray for the Rapture of true believers. Amen.

Show Us the Father

> "Philip saith unto him, 'Lord, shew us the Father, and it sufficeth us.' Jesus saith unto him, 'Have I been so long time with thou, and yet has thou not known me, Philip? He that hath seen me, hath seen the Father; and how sayest thou then, shew us the Father?'" (John 14:8, 9).

The Father, the Son, the Holy Ghost. These three are individuals, yet indivisible.

Have you ever known a man that had a son that looked just like his father? People would say, like father, like son or he's the spittin' image of his father. Now if they had a close relationship, the father would train the son in his ways and hobbies, like hunting, fishing, and sports but most importantly spiritual values, a moral code to live by would be passed down from the father to the son. If the father had his own business, that too he would pass down to his son. His son would be his representative and overseer of his business when he was not there. What Jesus is saying in these verses to Philip is, I have the same values as my Father, therefore there is no need to search for more than Myself because if you were to talk to God, the Father, He would say, "Listen to My Son, he represents me perfectly in every way." Why? Because he is my only begotten Son and I trained Him to be just like me. We existed together from the beginning in heaven. The Holy Ghost is the means of communication with much comfort to give. Amen.

Why, Judas, Why?

> "And after the sop, Satan entered into him. Then
> said Jesus unto him, That thou doest, do quickly"
> (John 13:27).

Judas walked with Jesus and the other eleven disciples for three years. Judas was a Christian, so what happened? Why did he betray Jesus? Judas was not totally committed to being a Christian so he did not have a hedge of protection around his spirit. He also carried the money bag for the group. Judas was not a terrible person; he just gave into temptation. As to why Judas betrayed Jesus, we can only speculate. He could have been taking money out of the money bag and needed to replace it before Matthew did an audit. I say Matthew because He was a tax collector before he was called to the ministry by Jesus. So Judas may have reasoned that for thirty pieces of silver he could replace the money that he stole. As for turning in Jesus, Judas thought that Jesus would be forced to handle the situation by a display of His power and after the smoke cleared, Judas would say he was sorry and say, "Okay! Way to go, Jesus! I knew you could do it." But whatever the reasoning that motivated Judas to betray Christ, the sad reality was Judas was so devastated by his sin that he hung himself. Judas didn't know that Jesus came into the world to be the sacrificial lamb to die for us on the cross. Had Judas grasped the meaning of the saving grace, which would come after the crucifixion of Jesus, then perhaps he would have repented of his sin of letting Satan guide him to do his bidding. Instead of killing himself, he could have continued in the ministry and eventually die as a martyr like most of the other apostles. Satan has led millions down a road to a life of hopelessness and despair, from a high to a low, so low that they enter a death spiral from which they can't escape.

> "No man can serve two masters: for either he will
> hate the one, and love the other; or else he will
> hold to the one, and despise the other. Ye cannot
> serve God and mammon" (Matt. 6:24).

Lord Jesus, protect us from the evil plans of Satan. Amen.

Money

> "And He said unto them, take nothing for your
> journey, neither staves, nor script, neither bread,
> neither money; neither have two coats" (Luke 9:3).

A lot has happened since Jesus walked this earth. The apostles had to really walk by faith. It is hard to imagine taking a trip without bringing along some money. They were totally dependent on God providing their substance through the peoples they visited.

I can't imagine Jesus coming to earth today and telling his apostles to go on television and ask for money so they can spread the Gospel. If money is so important to the spreading of the Gospel, then Jesus would have had Judas divide the money he was holding in the money bag to the apostles or He could have had fish bring gold coins to them so they were wealthy on their journey.

I have heard TV preachers wanting people to pledge thousands of dollars to their ministry, then later reading a report of how they are living like kings off the very same monies that they begged for—and all in the Name of Jesus! Woe unto those that use the name of Christ to get riches. You will answer to God for every penny you spend. Amen.

We need money to live in this present economic system in America. That is why we use the opportunity we have to work hard and prosper. We need to ask God for wisdom to manage our money so we don't waste or over spend. The Bible has a lot to say about money. Here are some Bible verses:

> "And he saith unto them, 'Whose is this image and
> superscription?' They say unto him, 'Caesar's.'
> Then saith he unto them, 'Render therefore unto
> Caesar the things which are Caesar's; and unto
> God the things that are God's'" (Matt. 22:20–21).
>
> "And there came a certain poor widow, and
> she threw in two mites, which make a farthing.
> And he called unto him his disciples, and saith
> unto them, 'Verily I say unto you, That this poor

widow hath cast more in, than all they which have cast into the treasury: For all they, did cast in of their abundance; but she of her want did cast in all that she had, even all her living'" (Mark 12:42–44).

"But Peter said unto him, 'Thy money perish with thee, because thou has thought that the gift of God may be purchased with money'" (Acts 8:20).

"For the love of money is the root of all evil: which while some coveted after, they have erred from the faith, and pierced themselves through with many sorrows" (1 Tim. 6:10).

"Riches profit not in the day of wrath: but rightousness delivereth from death" (Prov. 11:4).

"Go to now ye rich men, weep and howl for your miseries that shall come upon you. Your riches are corrupted, and your garments are moth eaten" (James 5:1).

Wisdom

"But the wisdom that is from above is first pure, then peaceable, gentle and easy to be entreated, full of mercy and good fruits, without partiality, and without hypocrisy" (James 3:17).

"For the wisdom of this world is foolishness with God. For it is written, He taketh the wise in their own craftiness" (1 Cor. 3:19).

There are two kinds of wisdom: one is from God and is pure; the other is worldly and comes from man's intellect but is really foolishness.

Some people strive for higher levels of education. They are honored by wearing large robes and hats. They pride themselves in their collection of degrees. They stand up for diversity and being liberal in respecting all manner of evil lifestyles. Some call evil good and good evil; and they think they are wise in their own eyes but have become fools.

The fear of God is the beginning of wisdom. Then add to fear, purity, and love of God and diligent study of the Bible. The King James Version is best. He or she that obeys God's commandments not to sin is wise with godly wisdom that is better than gold.

> "Then shalt thou understand the fear of the Lord,
> and find the knowledge of God" (Prov. 2:5).

Help us find wisdom, Lord Jesus! Amen.

America

> "If any man defile the temple of God, him shall
> God destroy; for the temple of God is holy, which
> temple are ye" (1 Cor. 3:17).

America! Land of the free? Free to do what? Live in sin! Change the laws of the government to accommodate those members of society to live in sin and not be held guilty. Free to allow all kinds of false religions to enter into our country. Free to practice witchcraft, sorcery, and every form of anti-God craft.

America the Great! How low can you go? Every sinful law that has been passed, from abortion on demand to homosexuals getting married, has all been done in the name of freedom for all.

Our founding fathers would be turning in their graves if they could see us now, but they made the mistake of leaving out Jesus Christ as the cornerstone in the foundation of our country. They prayed to God but left out Christ. That is why some of our founding fathers were slave owners and fathered children by their slaves. If you call yourself a Christian and do not have love for others, then you are Christian by name only, which has no power to save. The word *God* is just a title that can be applied to whatever we want our God to be. Even an atheist is a believer in God, not the true God, but the God of self, becoming a slave to their own intellect, which is sin. In the

Declaration of Independence in 1776, they refer to God as "nature's God." And in the Bill of Rights, Congress is prohibited from making laws establishing religion. By doing this they opened the Pandora's box to say, "Anything goes."

So how do we define the one and only true God? In the Bible, God is called by different names, such as Jehovah God, Lord, the great I AM. But the main identifier is when Jesus called God, Father. And in Mark 14:36, Jesus prayed, saying, "Abba, Father, all things are possible unto thee." Also in John 14:9, Jesus said to Phillip, "He that hath seen me hath seen the Father." And Jesus said in John 14:11, "Believe in me that I am in the Father, and the Father in Me." So I conclude that the only true God has to be all inclusive with Jesus Christ and no other name.

The true Christians in America are the only thing that is stopping the destruction of God's judgment on America. When Christ is taken out of America, then the apple will be completely rotten to the core. True Christians look forward to the Rapture of the church, the body of believers that are prepared to meet Jesus in the air at the sound of the last trump and the voice of the archangel saying, "Come up hither," where we will be forever with the Lord.

Jesus, come save us from destruction! Amen.

Many Deceivers

> "For many shall come in My Name, saying, I am
> Christ; and shall deceive many" (Matt. 24:5).

There are men that actually claim to be Jesus Christ, and as crazy as it sounds, they actually have a following. The Bible warns us not to be deceived by anyone that claims to be Jesus Christ. This is the most obvious and easy way to recognize examples of what Jesus warns us about.

There is another example of a type of false Christ in the world that we as Christians need to be aware of. The best way to identify a false image of Jesus Christ is to get to know Him personally. It is called being born again. Now once you are born again and chosen to live your life for God, you need to study the Bible. The best place to start reading the Bible is in the Gospel of John. As you read, meditate on the red letter words, which are the words of Christ. As you read, picture in your mind Jesus speaking as if you are there and the Holy Spirit will confirm with your spirit the true Jesus. There is much power in the Word of God. Amen.

God's Words

"He that is of God heareth God's words: ye therefore hear them not, because ye are not of God" (John 8:47).

"Jesus said unto them, If God were your Father, ye would love me: for I proceeded forth and came from God; neither came I of myself, but He sent me" (John 8:42).

Jesus himself was that standard by which we can judge who or what can qualify as being from the one true God.

If Jesus Christ is not the center of one's faith, then they are of the devil. Knowing this important fact is to be in agreement with Jesus, and there is no other that I would put before Jesus.

I suggest you read all of John chapter 8 to get a better understanding of what Jesus is saying to the Jews here.

People of worldly wisdom would like to believe that there are many paths that all lead to God and heaven, but the truth is there is only one path and it is straight and narrow.

I would estimate that those that are on that narrow path that Jesus told us about are very few indeed. Because of what Jesus said, the number of people saved are in the millions in a world of billions. I would say less than 10 percent of all peoples. This is why we should help spread the gospel to the world. Amen.

A Time of Testing

> "Now the brother shall betray the brother to
> death, and the father the son; and children shall
> rise up against their parents, and shall cause them
> to be put to death" (Mark 13:12).

In order to understand the meaning of this verse, we need to realize that Jesus is speaking about what it will be like in the world, in the very last days before He returns to judge the last generation on earth.

I predict that in the last days, there will be a world government that will totally control and monitor all aspects of people's lives. And just like Hitler blamed the Jews for Germany's financial problems, the New World Order will turn its focus on Christians. The news will be controlled and spew out Antichrist propaganda. The children will be taught an Antichrist, humanistic religion in school. There will be an economic collapse due to greedy people controlling the government and finances. The news will blame the Christians for the collapse, and the government will make Christianity a crime punishable by death, just like the Roman Empire did. Children will be paid by the schools to report their parents to the authorities for having a Bible in the home.

How many Christians will be able to stand up to this kind of persecution? Help us, Jesus! Amen.

Why the Narrow Path?

> "And ye shall be hated of all men for my name's
> sake: but he that shall endure unto the end, the
> same shall be saved" (Mark 13:13).

When you asked Jesus to come into your heart and transform your thinking to line up with his commandments, you had no idea what your future would be.

Let's face it, no one wants to be hated. We live in a world where it's not popular to hate or be hated. Everyone wants to be accepted as they are. Sin is something to be proud of in this sin-sick society of America 2010. Now it's 2018, and I see these things happening now.

If a true Christian is one who loves their neighbors, feeds the hungry, spreads the good news of salvation to the lost world, and speaks the truth in love, then why does the world hate them so?

Because the world hated Jesus. The devil hates Jesus. The Word of God cuts to the bone. The light of Christ exposes sin as evil. Sin is unacceptable and has no place in the Kingdom of God. Those that hate Christians are in love with the world and love their sins. Those that find Christ and walk the narrow path find everlasting life and freedom from sin. Amen.

A True Convert

> "The law of the Lord is perfect, converting the soul: the testimony of the Lord is sure, making wise the simple" (Ps. 19:7).
>
> "And said, 'Verily I say unto you, except ye be converted, and become as little children, ye shall not enter into the kingdom of heaven'" (Matt. 18:3).

You don't hear the word *converted* very often today. It has been replaced by words like *born again* and *saved*. How many people do you know that have been converted? I don't mean someone that is in recovery from alcohol or drugs. I mean, who do you know that has truly been converted by the power of God? I'm talking about a transformation from being one way to completely different in speech, actions, habits and someone that loves God with a zeal for reading the Word.

I know a few, and they have been a blessing to me. I feel a bond that is like a brother or sister but in a different way, a spiritual bond that is hard to put into words. This bond that Christians share is the knowing in the spirit, that we are a part of something that is bigger than the total sum of all the parts put together. That is because when you bring together a group of born-again believers, Jesus Christ is there in the midst. You can sense His Holy Spirit and His presence.

The reason Jesus said, "Ye must be like these children," is because once you are truly converted, you develop an innocence and a hope and faith in believing something that can't be seen. It's like believing in Santa Clause when you were a child and waiting with expectations of wonderful things on Christmas Eve. The big difference is that God and Jesus Christ are real, and when we die, we will not be disappointed. That day will be a million times greater than Christmas morning!

The world has a lot of evil, but it doesn't have to be that way. If everyone could put aside their differences, lay down their weapons, and receive Jesus with the faith of a child, the world could be a beautiful place, just as God intended it to be. Today I pray for peace, love, and an end to the killing. Life begins at conception and should end at a ripe old age. Amen.

Joy Unspeakable

> "Likewise, I say unto you there is joy in the presence of the angels of God over one sinner that repenteth" (Luke 15:10).
>
> "My brethren, count it all joy when ye fall into diverse temptations" (Luke 15:10).

There is something going on in the spiritual realm that we cannot see, but I can feel it in my spirit.

Why would God's angels be full of joy when a sinner repents? Why should the Christian be joyful when being tested by temptations?

> "Not for that we have dominion over your faith, but are helpers of your joy: for by faith ye stand" (2 Cor. 1:24).

It takes faith to walk the narrow path. I believe there is an awesome future reward for those that seek God's righteousness and apply those things to live a life pleasing to God.

I believe we will receive immortal bodies that feel no pain, perfect health, perfect teeth, strong bones and muscles, able to walk through walls and travel at the speed of light, anywhere in the universe.

It all makes sense to me now that I think about the eternal possibilities. After all, God isn't going to entrust anyone with eternal life that would use that power for evil. Why should He? We have enough devils to deal with now; we certainly don't need any more.

So here you have it, true repentance as set forth by Jesus Christ is the only way for a man to be saved. Why? Because man sees only the outward appearance of man but Jesus resides in your heart and knows your every thought. You can't fool Jesus. The bottom-line is this: Jesus is not going to reward a hypocrite and a liar and all other manner of sinners with a beautiful heavenly mansion with angels and an immortal Superman-type body.

That is why there is so much joy in heaven when a sinner repents. It's because there will be joy unspeakable when we get to heaven. I don't fear death anymore. If or when I die, don't cry over my mortal body. Just rejoice with the angels and praise God for His Son, Jesus, because without Jesus laying down his life for us, we could never have eternal life.

Thank you, Jesus! Amen.

Being Steadfast

> "For we are made partakers of Christ, if we hold the beginning of our confidence steadfast unto the end" (Heb. 3:14).
>
> "Neither is there any creature that is not manifest in his sight; but all things are naked and opened unto the eyes of Him with whom we have to do" (Heb. 4:13).

It is so easy to become lazy and stop going to church. The devil is always whispering in our ear to stay home, sleep in, don't give your money to the church. But God wants us to be steadfast in doing His will. There are reasons why we cannot fully understand the big picture that only God sees. There is much happening in the spirit world that we cannot see.

> "For now we see through a glass, darkly; but then
> face to face: now I know in part; but then shall I
> know even as also I am known" (1 Cor. 13:12).

Everything that we do or sacrifice for the Lord has so much importance to our benefit and the benefit of others that we just don't understand now, but we will someday.

To be steadfast with the Lord is to be unshakeable, unmovable, and ultimately raised up immortal and indestructible. There is no little things done when it comes to Jesus. Everything that has a heavenly purpose is eternal and indestructible.

So get up and go to church and expect good things in the Name of Jesus. Amen.

Godly Wisdom

> "Neither their silver or their gold shall be able
> to deliver them in the day of the Lord's wrath;
> but the whole land shall be devoured by the fire
> of His jealousy: for He shall make even a speedy
> riddance of all them that dwell in the land"
> (Zeph. 1:18).

I have noticed over the years that every time there are financial problems, such as a recession, depression, or a real estate bubble burst, there are many advertisements offering to sell gold. They say that in unsure financial times the only thing you can count on is gold, as it holds its value. As a result of these advertisements, I am sure there are many people buying gold coins, and as of this date (2/21/10), they are selling at over $1,000.00 per one ounce coin. I am sure that those that sell these coins are making a nice profit.

I have heard of certain people that are hunkered down in their fortresses with a safe full of gold and silver coins, plenty of food, and guns with lots of ammunition. They are ready to ride out those terrible days ahead. They are called extreme preppers. These preppers are relying on material things, but the Bible tells us to call on God and pray for His provision and protection in our time of trouble. I do believe in being somewhat prepared but not to the point of being obsessed with worry. It is more important to be right with God and spiritually prepared than it is to have material goods stored up for the last days.

The Bible speaks of a day when all the earthly preparation will do no good. The best preparation is spiritual. Draw close to Jesus. Don't you know that all the riches of the world cannot erase one sin? One drop of Jesus's blood is worth all the riches of the earth and more; for by His blood we are forgiven, cleansed, and delivered from all sin. There is too much focus on forgiveness of sin and not enough preaching on being delivered from the reoccurring sins. Amen.

Do Not Borrow

> "The rich ruleth over the poor, and the borrower
> is servant to the lender" (Prov. 22:7).

It is always best to save your money and pay cash for what you need. This takes self-discipline and a mind that is focused on the narrow path, but once you learn some basic principles, you will be better off. The first principle rule to learn is the word *no*. Practice saying no to salesmen, bankers, investment advisors, your wife, your kids, yourself, and sometimes needy charities at church and in the community. Let's face it, if you give to every one that has their hand out, you won't have enough to pay your own bills.

You don't need to drive a new car or live in a fancy, expensive house. You don't need to eat out in fancy restaurants and wear fancy clothes. I bought a used van for $4,000.00. Paid cash. That means no monthly payments for years and years. If I bought a new van, it would have cost about $35,000, and with interest added on the cost, it would be about $45,000. It doesn't look pretty, but it gets me around.

Jesus preached be content with having the basic necessities in life. The TV commercials are just another form of mind control that works. That is why companies spend millions of dollars for a one minute slot during the Superbowl game.

Now save up enough money for a down payment on a house. A house is the only thing you should borrow money for because they are so expensive, but you could buy a two-family house and rent out one apartment for enough rent to pay your monthly mortgage payment.

But, if you want a single family home, get a fifteen-year mortgage and don't let your monthly payment exceed what you earn in one week's paycheck.

Now you will need a credit card to reserve hotel rooms, plane tickets, etc., but pay off the balance each month. Beware of the credit card trap. Owing a large balance takes forever to pay off and can be a nightmare.

God wants to bless you; but you have to be prudent; wise; thrifty; diligent; hardworking; a saver, not a borrower. Pay your offering to your church and look for ways to save money. Clip coupons, buy used, wait and pray before making large purchases.

Remember, it is sin to covet what others have, to envy others, to be materialistic, and to show off.

Help us, Lord, be satisfied with what we can afford. Amen.

Be Purified

> "Seeing ye have purified your souls in obeying the truth through the Spirit unto unfeigned love of the brethren, see that ye love one another with a pure heart fervently: Being born again, not of corruptible seed, but of incorruptible, by the Word of God, which liveth and abideth forever" (1 Pet. 1:22, 23).

Be purified! How? By obeying the truth through the Spirit.

Be born again! How? By the Word of God.

You must turn away from all sin, not just what is easy and convenient at the time.

In order to purify water, it must be heated until it boils at 212 degrees Fahrenheit. To purify gold, it must be heated until it melts into a liquid and skim off the dross. This is a process.

If God says in His Word that an adulterer (also the wicked and sexually immoral) shall not enter His kingdom, then that is what he means.

Now the question to be asked is, how does God know who does what? Well, it is safe to say that God knows all things, even our thoughts. So if that is true, then it makes sense that we must be born again and be purified. We need to flood our mind with His Word and resist the devil. We need to fight the battle for our soul until we win. Losing and giving up is not an option.

> "I have fought a good fight, I have finished my
> course, I have kept the faith" (2 Tim. 4:7).

God knows how many hairs are on your head. If you are bald, God knows how many hairs are missing from your head.

If you go to hell, it's because you did not purify yourself. Don't blame God for what you failed to do. If you want to go somewhere, you have to buy a ticket to get in. If you want to join a club, you have to pay your dues to be a member and you have to abide by the rules to be a member in good standing. You can say you are a member and know all the rules pertaining to members, but if you don't pay your dues, you will not be allowed in the door.

Do you think that just because you say prayers and go to church that God is going to overlook your sins? Did Jesus ever say, "Don't worry about your sins, you can enter My Kingdom" or "I don't mind that you are a wicked, evil person. Come on in anyway."

Read the Bible! Amen.

Evil Spirits of Alcohol

> "Nor thieves, nor covetous, nor drunkards, nor
> revilers, nor extortionists shall inherit the king-
> dom of God" (1 Cor. 6:10).

If alcohol, an addictive drug, is packaged and sold to the public, you must ask the question, why? The answer is, it's all about the money.

Beer, wine, whiskey, vodka, gin—they all have alcohol. How many people die each year in alcohol-related accidents on our roads? How many people are killed, shot, stabbed, beat up, assaulted, raped because of alcohol? How many families are destroyed? How many jobs are lost and accidents at work or at home because of alcohol?

If you drink, you need to quit. If you work in the industries that manufacture alcoholic drinks, you need to find another job. If you own stocks or mutual funds that are invested in these factories, breweries, you need to sell them. Don't you know that it is all blood money? You will answer to God on judgment day.

Wake up, America! Stop the brainwashing. The actors in the beer commercials are so young and beautiful and happy. What they don't show are the dead bodies, the alcoholic stupor, the DTs of withdrawal, the children crying because Daddy is hurting Mommy. Wake up, my people, and walk the narrow path. I pray that your eyes will be opened to the truth. Amen.

Protect Your Body

> "I beseech you, therefore, brethren, by the mer-
> cies of God, that ye present your bodies a living
> sacrifice, holy, acceptable unto God, which is
> your reasonable service." (Rom. 12:1).

Alcohol, tobacco, drugs, fatty foods, sexually transmitted diseases, overwork, stress, worry— these are all destructive to our bodies and our minds and our spirits. "Wake up, my people," says the Lord.

Do not be deceived by the money changers. They care not for your life, only your money.

God wants us to live as healthy as possible. Don't think you can smoke for thirty years and then ask God to heal you of lung cancer. The Bible teaches us that we will reap what we sow. Remember the billion-dollar campaigns to brainwash the people and lead them like sheep to the slaughterhouses? Why? All for the love of money. It's a big money machine that thrives on sickness, addictions, death and destruction from the barrooms to the casinos, the illegal drug dealers to the pharmaceutical giants. The doctors and the lawyers also profit from sickness and disease. They will spend millions to protect animals but will throw people in a garbage dumpster and say, "They were never born. What value are they? It's just a fetus. It's so small and not formed yet."

I was once a fetus, and so were you.

Thank God my loving mother didn't have an abortion or I wouldn't be writing this book.

Not a fetus, but a human being with a soul, created in the image of God. At last count, there have been 63,000,000 people murdered in abortion clinics in America. I wonder how many would have grown up to be a pastor or prophet or a scientist that could find a cure for cancer.

Father, Stop the Genocide! Amen.

> "Their bows also shall dash the young men to pieces; and they shall have no pity on the fruit of the womb; there eye shall not spare children" (Isa. 13:18).
>
> "As thou knowest not what is the way of the spirit, nor how the bones do grow in the womb of her that is with child: even so thou knowest not the works of God who maketh all' (Eccles. 11:5).
>
> "Before I formed thee in the belly I knew thee; and before thou camest forth out of the

womb I sanctified thee, and I ordained thee a prophet before the nations" (Jer. 1:5).

"Jerusalem, Jerusalem, thou that killest the prophets, and stonest them which are sent unto thee, how often would I have gathered thy children together, even as a hen gathereth her chickens under her wings, but ye would not!" (Matt. 23:37).

"For, behold, the days are coming, in the which they shall say, Blessed are the barren, and the wombs that never bare, and the paps which never gave suck" (Luke 23:29).

"Then shall they begin to say to the mountains, Fall on us; and to the hills, Cover us" (Luke 23:30).

"Behold, your house is left unto you desolate" (Matt. 23:38).

The Rapture!

"Behold, I shew you a mystery; we shall not all sleep, but we shall all be changed. In a moment, in the twinkling of an eye, at the last trump: for the trumpet shall sound, and the dead shall be raised incorruptible, and we shall be changed" (1 Cor. 15:51, 52).

"For the Lord himself shall descend from heaven with a shout, with the voice of the archangel, and with the trump of God: and the dead in Christ shall rise first: Then we which are alive and remain shall be caught up together with them in the clouds to meet the Lord in the air; and so shall we ever be with the Lord" (1 Thess. 4:16, 17).

"Two women shall be grinding at the mill; the one shall be taken, and the other left" (Matt. 24:41).

"For as a snare shall it come on all them
that dwell on the face of the whole earth. Watch
ye, therefore, and pray always that ye may be
accounted worthy to escape all these things that
shall come to pass, and to stand before the Son of
Man" (Luke 21:35, 36).

Jesus gives us warning after warning to stay awake, be sober, be watchful, and be expecting of His return any day. He also tells us to pray that we will be found worthy when He returns. I am not taking any chances because I don't want to be counted as being unworthy and miss the Rapture. When that last trumpet sounds, I hope it happens when I am in church, praying or reading my Bible.

I thank God for delivering me from evil habits. This is no joke. This is serious stuff. Jesus said that His return would be swift and be like a snare on everyone in the world at the same time. That tells me that due to twenty-four time zones, many will be asleep when He returns. Let's hope they will be sleeping alone, or with their spouse. What if Jesus comes on a Friday or Saturday night, where will you be? What will you be doing?

"Watch therefore, for ye know neither the day
nor the hour wherein the Son of Man cometh"
(Matt. 25:13).

Lord Jesus, sanctify us! Protect us! And lead us not into temptation. Amen.

Hell's Gates

"And I say also unto thee, that thou art Peter, and
upon this rock I will build my church; and the gates
of hell shall not prevail against it" (Matt. 16:18).

There are many gates that give access to hell. Anything that has a handle or knob or buttons whereby we access another reality, such as a television, radio, computer. These can be opened or closed to another reality.

When you open a DVD case, it is hinged like a gate. Have you noticed that the movies are getting worse every year? Some are full of evil, witchcraft, demons, devils, fortune telling, spell casting and all manner of blasphemy. And I am talking about PG-13 rated movies. Everywhere you go in the malls, it seems that skulls and demons are the latest style. You see them printed on T-shirts, jackets, purses. Could this be a way to condition this generation so they will not be afraid of Satan and his demons or to welcome the Antichrist?

Now listen carefully, you Christians, once you pray for a hedge of protection, you have to stop opening hell's gates and inviting evil to enter your mind. Your home should be a sanctuary. Lay down the rules and hold up a standard in your home. I pray for protection against all evil in Jesus's Name. Amen.

Gabbatha (The Pavement)

> "Then delivered he him therefore unto them to be crucified and they took Jesus and led him away" (John 19:16).

From John 18:28 until John 19:13, Pilate found no guilt in Jesus in the Judgment Hall, but something happened. In John 19:12, the Jews made Jesus's trial into a political worry that could threaten Pilate's career. The Jews turned Jesus's trial for blasphemy against God into a political crime against Caesar. It was then that Jesus was taken from the Judgment Hall to Gabbatha, the pavement. There Pilate sat on a different judgment seat. It was at Gabbatha where Pilate changed his judgment of Jesus from innocent to guilty—all because he wanted to be politically correct.

Christians, wake up! Go back to your first love of Christ and His holy judgments of good and evil. Don't be persuaded by pressures to be politically correct.

Just like Pilate's mind was turned, so is America's moral fiber. What was once considered to be an abomination is now considered to be politically correct and socially acceptable. What once made the angels cry, now make the devils laugh! Jesus, save us from moral destruction! Amen.

Adultery

> "He that is without sin among you, let him first cast a stone at her" (John 8:7).

Read John 8:1–12. This verse in the Bible is probably the most quoted verse by sinners trying to justify their sinful lifestyle. It is the sinner that quotes this verse to the Christian that is trying to rebuke their sin. Let me say that whenever someone quotes this verse out of desperation, that it is the devil speaking through them.

Jesus's whole purpose here is to end the needless killing and to show the scribes and Pharisees that it was time to show mercy by the grace of God. This also showed the scribes and Pharisees that they were guilty of sin in their own lives.

To properly understand what is happening here, you have to read John 8:1–12. In verse 4 she is guilty; verse 5, she is condemned to death; verse 7, she finds mercy; verse 10, her sentence of death is dismissed; verse 11, she receives God's forgiveness and cleansing and is told to sin no more. In verse 12, Jesus explains how she can walk the narrow path.

The devil likes to leave out verse 11, "*Go and sin no more!*" Why? Because the devil is a crafty liar. He goes around trying to mislead Christians into thinking it's okay to live in sin. Well, that is not true. We all must deal with sin in our lives.

Please, Lord, convict us of our sins so we can be set free! Amen.

Lust

> "For all that is in the world, the lust of the flesh, the lust of the eyes, and the pride of life, is not of the Father, but is of the world" (1 John 2:16)

> "These be they who separate themselves;
> sensual, having not the Spirit" (Jude 19).

Lust is a "sexual desire as a sensual degrading passion" according to the dictionary.

Lust is a demonic spirit that invades a person's spirit. Once in place, the person needs to repent and be delivered and set free. Lust is not to be confused with love or the act of sexual love between a husband and wife. These are two different acts. The act of lust is evil and from the devil. The act of sexual love between the husband and wife is good and God-ordained. God created Adam and Eve, not Adam and Steve!

Lord Jesus, cleanse and deliver us all from lust! Amen.

Jesus Is a Virgin

> "And I looked and lo, a Lamb stood on Mount Sion, and with him an hundred forty and four thousand, having his Father's name written in their foreheads" (Rev. 14:1).
>
> "These are they which were not defiled with women; for they are virgins. These are they which follow the Lamb withersoever he goeth. These were redeemed from among men, being the first fruits unto God and to the Lamb" (Rev. 14:4).

There is a blasphemy circulating by some writers saying Jesus had sex with Mary Magdalene, and some say Jesus had homosexual relations with the apostles. When I heard this, I felt physically sick. All I have to say to those that are spreading this lie is, woe unto you!

Now for the truth: Jesus was all man, not a wimp. He was also God in the flesh and was our perfect example. As a perfect example, Jesus controlled all fleshly desires and emotions. Jesus remained a virgin, and those that devoted their lives to serve Christ, many have remained virgins their entire life.

One of Satan's tools is sexual lust. This is a most destructive sin that has ruined many lives and sent many to hell. Sex was meant to be between a man and woman, husband and wife, mainly for procreation, as the Bible says, to replenish the earth.

The Bible also tells husband and wife to abstain from sex for a period of time to draw closer to God. The world could use more people that feel led to remain virgins.

Look at the 144,000 virgin men of God in the book of Revelation. They held a very special position in God's kingdom. They were certainly a very special group as they were first-fruits unto God and Jesus. There were women that remained virgins and devoted themselves to God, and they too have a special place and reward in heaven.

There is something special about the holiness of those that choose to remain celibate to serve God. It shows self-control. The world needs more of this kind of example for the children. The government should outlaw all types of Internet pornography before it corrupts a whole generation.

Lord Jesus, come back soon and rule the world your way, the right way, the holy way! Amen.

Spiritual Gold

> "I counsel thee to buy of me gold tried in the fire, that thou mayest be rich; and white raiment that thou mayest be clothed, and that the shame of thy nakedness do not appear; and anoint thy eyes with eye salve, that thou mayest see. As many as I love, I rebuke and chasten: be zealous, therefore, and repent!"(Rev. 3:18, 19).

There is a spiritual type of gold and white robes that can be bought from Jesus Christ, but these cannot be bought with money. Everything that Jesus is talking about here has to do with things of the spirit—His Spirit, the Holy Spirit, our spirit. Gold tried in the fire is the condition of our spirit after overcoming the trials and tribulations of this life. This is only in the context of living and suffering the Christian life with rejection of and by the things of the world. Our flesh can ignite a fire that tries to consume the spirit. But the more that fire rages, the more the spirit is refined like gold. All this is only possible when we go to Christ as our counselor and repent of our sins. Repent with a zealous heart toward God and all his commandments. Do not be bitter when God rebukes and chastens you. Rejoice because that means He loves you! Amen.

Born Again?

Being born again is not to be taken lightly. To be truly born again, first, there needs to be conviction of the sinful nature, then a desire to repent and ask God for His forgiveness, His mercy, and His anointing. Then you need to get water baptized as a public announcement of wanting to be a Christian, then Bible studies to learn how to survive as a Christian.

I have seen some ministries that say, "Just say the sinner's prayer." A prayer that has been pre-printed and needs to be recited, and after you repeat the prayer, then you are saved.

Well, I have a problem with that! When we study God's Word, Jesus said many things to the people. I don't find it anywhere in Jesus's teachings about being saved by repeating a prayer. Although I can see that the sinner's prayer would be a starting point of contact with Jesus, I think it is wrong to say to a new Christian that this is all that needs to be done to be saved. I challenge anyone to read the four Gospels and the book of Revelation and focus on the words of Christ. This is why I don't believe in "once saved always saved." That is a false gospel, and anyone that preaches a false gospel will be accursed, according to Galatians 1:8. If all that was necessary to be saved was to say the sinner's prayer, then why go to church on Sunday? Could this be one reason why so many churches today are losing members and closing down? We need preachers that are not afraid to call sin, sin and put the fear of God in people, the fear of burning in the eternal flames of hell. How can people fear God if they are told they can't lose their salvation and they won't go to hell? Is this not contrary to what was preached by Jesus?

The Christian walk is a narrow path. Don't be deceived!

> "Blessed are they that do His commandments that they may have right to the tree of life, and may enter in through the gates into the city. For without are dogs, and sorcerers, and whoremongers, and murderers and idolaters, and whosoever loveth and maketh a lie" (Rev. 22:14, 15).

God and Natural Law

> "Thus they provoked him to anger with their inventions: and the plague brake in upon them" (Ps. 106:29).

God established the law as a way to live. A blessing comes with obedience and curses with disobedience. God built into nature certain diseases as punishment for sinful choices. For every action there is a reaction. For every choice there is a consequence: good for good and bad for bad.

They say there are about 125 types of mushrooms, but only a few are safe to eat. Did you ever wonder how people knew which ones were safe to eat? How many people got sick or died testing the mushrooms? I bet the people that did wished that God would have warned them about the poison mushrooms.

God does warn us about other dangers by His laws in the Bible. For example, if everyone obeyed God and husbands and wives remained faithful to their spouse and the singles remained virgins, there would be no sexually transmitted diseases.

God's laws are there for our protection. Because of evil, however, man has invented ways to break God's laws without suffering the consequences. When the AIDS disease showed up about fifty years ago, they first told the homosexuals to practice safe sex, then put pressure on the government to find a cure. But when the Christian church told them to repent of their sin, they were ridiculed as being homophobic, judgmental, and uneducated. They wouldn't even consider celibacy. Why? Because they loved their sin more than God! Everything that God has made for us to enjoy as being good, the devil has turned into a curse for mankind. The good becomes a curse when it is misused outside the healthy boundaries of its intended purpose. This is where self-control is needed, where the fruit of the spirit is a sign of Christian maturity.

> "Wherefore by their fruits ye shall know them" (Matt. 7:20).
> "But the fruit of the Spirit is love, joy, peace, long-suffering, gentleness, goodness, faith, meekness, temperance: against such there is no law" (Gal. 5:22).

Lord, strengthen us! Amen.

Sin and Sickness

> "Behold, thou art made whole: sin no more, lest a worse thing come unto thee" (John 5:14).

A lot of sickness is a direct result of sin. Not all sickness, but quite a lot is due to sin.

The cost of health insurance is sky-high and rising. Why? Because there are so many people that are sick, and a lot of sickness is a direct result of living in sin. How many people die each year directly or indirectly from alcohol, tobacco, and drug abuse? It is a sin to pollute your body with these poisons. Once you accept Christ, your body becomes a temple for the Holy Spirit. Do not defile your body by abusing it.

A drug can become an addiction, but the first time you take the drug, it is a sin against your body. I believe that in order for an addict to find recovery, they first must admit they have sinned against God's laws and repent of their sinful lifestyle. Then they need to be gradually weaned off the drug. Teen Challenge has a very high success rate. It is a Christian, Bible-based recovery program.

Scientists work hard to find cures for diseases that can just be prevented by living the good life according to Christ's teachings. Sexually transmitted diseases are not a problem to those that are not living a life of sexual promiscuity. The schools would do better allowing God back in, instead of teaching children how to put a condom on a cucumber. Abstinence is the only way to be 100 percent safe from STDs. That is what the Bible teaches!

And what about the costs of damages to property and human life due to drunk drivers. Imagine a true Christian society! Car insurance: $25 per year. Health insurance: $100 per year.

There is an evil in our country that is growing like a cancer out of control. It is a double standard that is enslaving people. First by attacking the mind by enticing the senses through different types of mind control—television, movies, billboards, magazines, books, Internet, social media, music, etc. This leads the victim to covet that which will lead to their eventual destruction. These forms of mind control can lead to addiction to all types of evil, such as alcohol, tobacco, street drugs, prescription drugs, sweets, fast foods, overeating causing obesity, pornography, violence, racism, hatred, witchcraft, Satanism, risky sports, self-admiration, obsessive behavior, hoarding, love of money, gluttony, sexual lust.

> "For all that is in the world, the lust of the flesh, and the lust of the eyes, and the pride of life, is not of the Father, but is of the world" (John 2:16).
>
> "A man's pride shall bring him low: but honour shall uphold the humble in spirit" (Prov. 29:23).
>
> "For the iniquity of his covetousness was I wroth, and smote him: I hid me, and was wroth, and he went on frowardly in the way of his heart." (Isa. 57:17). Amen.

Sin and Sickness

> "That it might be fulfilled by which was spoken
> by Esaias the prophet, saying, Himself took our
> infirmities and bare our sicknesses" (Matt. 8:17).

When Jesus walked the earth, he started his ministry at age thirty and was crucified at age thirty-three. In those three years, He healed a lot of sickness. So why don't we see a lot of healings today? Probably because we don't see a lot of sinners repenting.

Most people do it all wrong. They wait until their lives are unmanageable due to alcohol and drugs, or they smoke for decades, refusing to quit until they start having health problems. Then they want Jesus to perform a miracle and heal their bodies after they abused themselves for years. The main reason they turn to Jesus is out of desperation. They want healing for their body but not their soul. They were told they are victims because they have an addiction by the so-called professionals. Well, it's time to wake up! Let's call using alcohol, tobacco, and drugs sinning against our bodies and against God; for it is written, we were made in the image of God! Amen.

> "For whom the Lord loveth, he chasteneth,
> and scourgeth every son whom he receiveth"
> (Heb. 12:6).

Read Hebrews 12:6–17.

After we correct our lifestyle to adjust to walking the narrow path of Christianity (such as not drinking, smoking, drugs, illicit sex,) and switching to a proper diet and exercise, we may find a sickness come on us from some other source. This sickness or infirmity may or may not be chastisement from God. If it is God's chastisement, we need to examine ourselves and seek God in prayer and fasting with a repentant heart. Ask God to show you, by the Holy Ghost conviction, what you are doing that is grieving the Holy Spirit. If you are married, it could be your spouse is in some sin causing chastisement to fall on you or from you to fall on your spouse. When you marry, two become one flesh. That is why the Bible says, do not be unequally yoked with an unbeliever. If you are living together and not married, go back to basic Christian morals. God will not bless that union. Repent and do whatever you have to until you are back in righteousness before God.

The Bible warns us of another cause of sickness. If you partake in Holy Communion in an unworthy state of unrepentant sin, you may become sick and die.

> "Thou hast not lied unto men, but unto God
> And Ananias hearing these words fell down, and
> gave up the ghost" (Acts 5:4–5).

Those who live with you, children, parents, friends can bring ungodly objects or influences into your home. That is why Job sacrificed offerings to God for the sins of his children. This is not a game! This is serious! Purge all evil from yourself and your home and pray for your friends and relatives.

Lord, open our eyes to be able to stand, for your Holiness is awesome! Amen.

Sin and Sickness

> "And I heard another voice from heaven saying,
> Come out of her my people, that ye be not par-
> takers of her sins, and that ye receive not of her
> plagues" (Rev. 18:4).

There is another cause of sickness and suffering. This is caused by sins of a corrupt society or nation. The Bible says that God is not a respecter of persons and He makes the rain to fall on the just as well as the unjust. The reason for this is because when a nation falls into sin, it is not only the fault of evil leadership, it is also due to the failure of Christians to stand up and take control of their government. In other words, good men and women of God are afraid to speak up against evil. Look at Sodom and Gomorrah. Yes, God saved Lot and his family, but had he refused to leave, then he and his family would have been destroyed also.

God sent Jonah to warn Nineveh's inhabitants to repent or be destroyed. The people of Nineveh were exceedingly wicked, but after Jonah told them that God would overthrow Nineveh after forty days, they believed God and they repented and were spared. Nineveh was a city of 120,000 and they all fasted and prayed in sackcloth and ashes. When the king saw this he did likewise.

Sin weakens a church, a person, a ministry, and a nation. Evil will rule for a time, but not forever. If there is a spiritual revolution, then the evil government will be overthrown. If not from within, then it will be from without. Jesus saves! Amen.

A Prophecy

Resist temptation to sin, and the devil will flee. Calm your soul in the peace and quiet. Pray for peace and wait upon the Lord. Listen to what the Holy Spirit has to say.

When the Twin Towers fell, the whole world watched in horror and awe. In an instant, destruction came and there was no way to stop it. All the information and technology that was already in place and operational did not prevent that evil from happening.

Do not put your trust in the technology to save you! Do not put your trust in your military to save you. Do not put your trust in money, gold or silver, provisions or fortresses to save your life in these last days.

When people turn their back on God and reject Jesus Christ and all that is holy, then they lose divine wisdom and protection. Like a drunkard that stumbles and gropes in the darkness to find the lock in the door, so it is with a nation that exalts sin and turns away from holiness. A people that think of sinful thoughts and wicked inventions night and day is a nation that has forgotten God. Unless there is a revival, that nation faces total destruction. Jesus said, "All authority has been given unto me." Who should we obey?

Supreme - highest in rank or authority

Supreme Court - the highest judicial tribunal in a nation

Supreme Being - God
Related Sins

> "And Jesus looked round about, and saith unto his disciples, 'How hardly shall they that have riches enter into the kingdom of God'" (Mark 10:23, 26).

Jesus Was Busy

> "And there are also many other things which Jesus did, the which if they should be written every one, I suppose that even the world itself could not contain the books that should be written. Amen." (John 21:25).

Jesus started his ministry when he was thirty years old, and he was crucified when he was thirty-three years old. That was only three years, but look at all he did in those three years! He changed the world, and it has been two thousand years since he was walking the earth, and millions of lives have been changed by the power of His Name.

Hollywood has produced many movies about Jesus, some good, some not so good. In all the movies produced, Jesus was portrayed as kind of laid-back and sitting on a rock or praying to God in the garden. All in all, I think that is an understatement as to how Jesus really was. I believe Jesus was very busy and a hard worker, toiling to serve mankind with a passion that we do not realize.

Think about how Jesus spread his good news of salvation. He walked or went by small boat. There were no cars, busses, trains, or planes. There were no televisions, computers, or cell phones for communication. There was no printed word, only that which was written by scribes on parchments.

Today we travel by car, plane, bus, or train and are enclosed in some sort of vehicle. Within that vehicle we are listening to music, talking on a cell phone, or watching videos and are isolated from others. It is possible to travel cross-country and not have conversation with anyone. Now imagine yourself walking across the country with twelve of your friends without any radio or iPod to distract you. Everywhere people will look at your group and ask questions. Who are you guys? Where are you coming from? Where are you going? A continual exchange of conversation, every day, everywhere you went. So vibrant, so alive! Even in conflict and persecution, never a dull moment. Are we becoming like the people of Nineveh in the book of Jonah that God said they could not discern between their right hand and their left hand? Is technology dumbing down America?

God is good! Praise Him always! Amen.

Jesus Saves Us

> "For the Son of man is not come to destroy men's lives, but to save them" (Luke 9:56).

Sometimes Christians look at all the evil around us, the constant bad news on TV, and we may say that God should destroy the evil people. Remember Sodom and Gomorrah and how God was willing to spare those cities if he could find ten good people.

Remember how we were before Jesus came into our lives? Where would we be today if God destroyed us before we received our salvation? Most likely we would be in hell with those people that were destroyed by God in times past.

Jesus came two thousand years ago to save people from their sinful lifestyle. To *save, forgive, deliver from, change direction, transform, be born again*—these are all words describing what happens when you receive Christ. If nothing happens, then there is only one reason why: you have not received Christ. So get out your Bible and immerse yourself in the Word, day and night, until you receive your salvation.

There must be evidence of a changed life. When Jesus returns, things will be changed. The lion will lay down next to the lamb and will eat straw. Now that is what I call evidence of change. Everyone must have a personal testimony of a changed life.

"But let none of you suffer as a murderer, or as a thief, or as an evildoer, or as a busybody in other man's matters. Yet if any man suffer as a Christian, let him not be ashamed; but let him glorify God on this behalf" (1 Pet. 4:15–18).

For the time has come that judgment must begin in the house of God, and if it first begin at us, what shall the end be of them that obey not the gospel of God? And if the righteous scarcely be saved, where shall the ungodly and the sinner appear?

Thank you, Jesus, for saving us! Amen.

Hate Yourself?

"If any man come to me and hate not his father and mother and wife, and children and brethren and sisters, yea and his own life also, he cannot be my disciple. And whosoever doth not bear his cross and come after me, cannot be my disciple" (Luke 14:26, 27).

After being born again, some Christians feel called into the ministry. Jesus warns those that want to be his disciple that they first should think things over and see if they have what it takes. This is not something to be taken lightly. There is also the possibility that persecution will come from family and friends. This is why Jesus said you may hate them. This is Jesus's way of saying, in a strong way, that God must come first in the life of the disciple. There is no room for debating over different beliefs that were handed down as traditions. Some are being called of God come out of diverse faiths and some out of idolatry. Some families had no religion and were worldly. These are obstacles the Christian has to overcome, not only in his own life but from his own family members. Verse 27 refers to the cross. That is persecution and death to self-desires that are fleshly and worldly.

Jesus leads by example. Let's follow! Amen.

Sin and Sickness

"And a certain man was there, which had an infirmity thirty and eight years" (John 5:5).

"Jesus saith unto him, rise, take up thy bed and walk" (John 5:8).

"Afterward, Jesus findeth him in the temple, and said unto him, Behold, thou art made whole: sin no more, lest a worse thing come unto thee" (John 5:14).

In the above Bible verses, Jesus implies that certain sicknesses are a result of sin. If we purge sin from our life, we can be sure of not contracting certain sickness but others may or may not be scientifically connected to sin. That is to say, that man, with all his knowledge, has yet to unlock the mysteries of the body or the universe.

To believe in Jesus is an act of faith. To follow Jesus and make his teachings our path in life takes faith with commitment. Only God knows what sickness we have been spared by being obedient to God's Word. And how about injuries due to accidents and violence? How many people are dead or paralyzed due to drunk drivers? There are many Bible verses that say that drunkenness is a sin. Sin is bad for your health!

"And take heed to yourselves, lest at any time your hearts be overcharged with surfeiting, and drunkenness, and cares of this life, and so that day come upon you unawares. For as a snare it shall come on all them that dwell on the face of the whole earth" (Luke 21:34–35)

Help us, Lord, to be sober and watching for your return. Amen.

The Enemy Within

> "And these are they which are sown among thorns; such as hear the word, And the cares of this world, and the deceitfulness of riches and the lusts of other things entering in, choke the word and it becometh unfruitful" (Mark 4:18, 19).

Sometimes we can be our own worst enemy when it comes to the Word of God. That is why we need to be careful what we let into our lives. We need to monitor our own thoughts and motives and be honest with ourselves. We need to sweep clean the floor of our mind with the spiritual broom of the Holy Spirit. We need to overcome the enemy within. The enemy wants to choke, suppress, smother, and stop the growth of the Word within our mind.

After we sweep clean our mind and find a place for the Word of God, then we can make godly decisions. What we decide will depend on how much value we place on God's Word and also our level of commitment to Jesus Christ, that is to say, how we view ourselves. Do you see yourself as an apostle or disciple of Christ? Do you see yourself as being a listener of Christ, like one of the five thousand that came out to see him when He fed the crowd with a few loaves and fishes? Or do you think you could have been like one of the crowd that were laying down their coats and waving palm branches as Jesus rode the colt into Jerusalem? Or do you think you could have been one of the crowd that cried out, "Crucify Him, crucify Him!"

Whatever your mind-set is, we all have a part to play. What part you will play depends on how well you read and memorize the script. If you skim over the Word, you may find yourself developing stage fright or you may not get the part you desired.

What you become in life is directly related to how much time and resources you invest into a certain area of life. If you work eighty hours a week to make money to buy things and go to church two or three times a year, your spiritual walk with God will be choked. As a result, you may fall into other evil temptations. Life is what you make it. Where are your priorities? Does God occupy a small corner in your mind, or is Christ in the center, keeping everything else in balance?

> "Judgment will I lay to the line, and righteous-
> ness to the plummet: and the hail shall sweep
> away the refuge of lies, and the waters shall over-
> flow the hiding place" (Isa. 28:17).

Breaking Sinful Habits

> "Is Israel a servant? Is he a home-born slave? Why
> is he spoiled?" (Jer. 2:14).

Once you receive Jesus Christ as your Lord, you have been adopted by Jesus and are a part of Israel, God's chosen people. Where the Bible refers to God speaking to Israel through a prophet or directly, take that for yourself as words of wisdom. Ask yourself, how can I use this in my own life?

As a child of God, we are not meant to be servants to sin. Do you feel like a slave in your own home? Time to break free from sinful habits! What do you repeat that is not pleasing to God? Do you go to the casino once a year? Play bingo at church once a week? Smoke a cigarette once an hour? Have a drink once a day?

Do these habits cause you to be short of cash? Can you not afford to pay God his due? Don't you see how sins of habit spoil your finances? God wants his children to be blessed and have an abundance. The devil comes to "kill, steal, and destroy" and to make us slaves and servants to him or his evil enterprises on this earth.

Break free, my brothers and sisters in Christ, for we are servants only to God and Jesus Christ. Break those evil habits! Amen.

Don't Deceive Yourself!

> "Let us therefore, as many as be perfect, be thus
> minded: and if in anything ye be otherwise
> minded, God shall reveal even this unto you...

For many walk of whom I have told you often,
and now tell you even weeping, that they are
the enemies of the cross of Christ: Whose end is
destruction, whose God is their belly, and whose
glory is in their shame, who mind earthly things"
(Phil. 3:15 and 3:18, 19)

If you put God first and study His word every day, Jesus Christ
will send the Holy Spirit and God will reveal those sinful ways in
your life. Not only will sin be revealed to your mind, you will be
made aware of bad choices you are about to make.

God requires us to live a sober life. Don't deceive yourself. Pray
and read your Bible, and God will reveal to you what you need to do
to be perfect in Christ. Amen.

Foolishness

"The thought of foolishness is sin: and the
scorner is an abomination to men" (Prov. 24:9).

Scorn means to reject with extreme contempt; emotion involving both anger and disgust.

As I read the words of Christ, I try to get a picture in my mind
of what was His personality. As I search the four gospels of Matthew,
Mark, Luke, and John and study Jesus's sayings and reactions, I have
formed an opinion as to His personality.

Jesus was loving and forgiving. He was also very serious.
Nowhere do I find any foolish talk or even any humor. Although
I am sure Jesus must have had some good times and he laughed on
occasion, the gospels record a man on a mission, all business, serious
about everything and every situation he encountered.

Jesus is my hero, and He is the example I wish to follow. He
was always in control of his emotions and his speech. Jesus's example is the opposite of the world. The world is full of foolishness, as
displayed in movies, television, theater, some art, and comedy. Some
radio talk shows are full of scorn aimed at our leaders today.

As people of God, we need to turn from all foolishness and scorn. We need to embrace wisdom, love, sound judgment and embrace peaceful dialogue with one another. This is the way to live in peace, not meaning any harm to anyone.

I believe that when Jesus cast out the money changers from the temple, he was in control of his emotions and didn't show anger, just displeasure, when he tipped over tables and the seats of those that sold doves. I believe this because after he cast them out, Jesus began healing the blind and the lame and the children were crying in the temple, "Hosanna to the Son of David."

The best way to protect ourselves and our churches from foolishness and scorn is to keep God's house a house of prayer rather than programs, to minister to the sick and pray for the sinners, to show love and self-control in our lives as an example to the world.

There is no place for foolishness in the body of Christ. While many Christians seek the gifts of the Holy Spirit, they are lax in growing the fruits of the spirit: love, joy, peace, long-suffering, gentleness, goodness, faith, meekness, temperance, and to crucify the flesh and walk in the Spirit. Amen.

Make Wise Choices

"The heart of the wise is in the house of mourning; but the heart of fools is in the house of mirth" (Eccles. 7:4).

"Be not among winebibbers, among riotous eaters of flesh: For the drunkard and the glutton shall come to poverty: and drowsiness shall clothe a man with rags" (Prov. 23:20, 21).

The world says, "Rejoice! Eat, drink, and be merry." The world is on the downward slide to death and destruction. The world doesn't acknowledge Jesus Christ as the only Son of God. These are they that are of the world. They have set up gods for themselves, fashioned after their own image. To worship God is to look in a mirror and say to their reflection, "I have my own belief, and I follow my own inner compass, wherever it will lead me." They are not aware of the adversary, Satan, who will lead them down the broad road to destruction.

Who is the man that needs no teacher? What kind of man is he that needs no Savior? We have all gone astray, like children lost in a forest. Who is man to say, "I have ascended to the heavens?"

We are lost and without direction all the days of our life if we do not give honor and glory to the King of kings and Lord of lords.

> "He that saith unto the wicked, thou art righteous, him shall the people curse, nations shall abhor him: But to them that rebuke him shall be delight, and a good blessing shall come upon them" (Prov. 24:24, 25).

> "As the thorn goeth up into the hand of a drunkard, so is a parable in the mouth of fools" (Prov. 26:9).

Humble thyself and seek the kingdom of God and His righteousness, and He will guide your path. Jesus said that there is a narrow gate and a path that leads to life everlasting and only a few will ever find that path and fewer still will be able to walk down that path. That is why we need to press in with Christ and forsake the ways of the world. Don't be afraid of persecutions when they come our way. Remember, God is in control and He will have his day of vengeance upon the wicked and ungodly. We need to focus on being obedient servants to the living Christ. Amen.

Jesus Heals

> "There came also a multitude out of the cities round about unto Jerusalem, bringing sick folks, and them which were vexed with unclean spirits: and they were healed every one" (Acts 5:16).

The healing power first came from Jesus, then through his apostles. If you go back and read Acts 5:1–15, Annanias and Sapphira tempted the Spirit of the Lord and they both dropped dead. After this, the people were afraid and then came much power. Enough power that the people were all healed, and the apostles were all with one accord.

The reason we don't see a lot of healings today is because the Christian church is not of one accord. The devil has caused division, and there is little fear of God.

Most church members are stingy when they should be generous. They say that 98 percent of church attendees gives only one percent of their income. I don't believe in giving a certain set percentage each week, but the Bible refers to 10 percent as a requirement in the Old Testament. And God loves a cheerful and generous giver. So if you want your church to be financially healthy, you need to be more generous. If you want to see healing again, then fear God and take your Christian walk down that narrow path. If you can't trust God with your finances, then you don't have enough faith for your healing. How can you say, God, heal me by performing a miracle when in your heart you believe that if you give the church 10 percent of your income, you won't have enough money left to survive? Is greed in your heart preventing you from giving more? Lord, heal us! Lord build up our faith. Amen.

Look at what is available to us today. We are so blessed to have the freedom to go to church without persecution. We have the Old and New Testament Bibles in an assortment of languages and translations. There are many Christian churches everywhere, as well as many Christian television shows, radio shows, CDs and DVDs. We are without excuse.

They Chose Barabbas

> "And they cried out all at once, saying 'Away with this man, and release unto us Barabbas.' Pilate therefore, willing to release Jesus, spake again to them. But they cried saying, 'Crucify Him, Crucify Him!'" (Luke 23:18, 20, 21).

Life is full of choices, and by our choices, we can be our own worst enemy. Once you make a bad choice, it's done. Too late to take it back and do it over. Now we must live with the consequences of our actions.

Look at Luke and read about the trial of Jesus. Anyone can see that Pilate found no guilt with Jesus, yet there was much hatred toward Jesus by the Jews. Pilate offered to release Jesus, but they wanted Barabbas, the murderer. They had three chances, by Pilate, to change their minds and have Jesus released; but they said, "No, crucify Him."

How many chances have you had to accept Jesus? How many times have you said, "No, give me someone or something else." Did you say no to Jesus and say yes to something that you thought would bring happiness or fulfillment to your life, then feeling empty, depressed, and unfulfilled? Like Barabbas, the devil is a murderer. How many on Judgment Day will wish they could go back and change their bad choices in life? Today is your day to make it right. Choose Jesus as Lord today!

> "Behold, now is the accepted time; behold, now is the day of salvation" (2 Cor. 6:2).

All Have Sinned

> "And I wept much because no man was found worthy to open and to read the book, neither to look thereon" (Rev. 5:4).
>
> "He that overcometh, the same shall be clothed in white raiment; and I will not blot out his name out of the book of life, but I will confess his name before my father, and before his angels" (Rev. 3:5).

No one can stand before Christ and say they have never sinned. We all fall short. But what determines who will be saved and who will be condemned is the living and active Christ working within us; for He is worthy, the Lion of the Tribe of Judah, our Lord, Jesus Christ.

I have read the Bible from cover to cover, and I know how the story ends. The devil will be chained up for one thousand years, then Satan and all his demons will be cast into the lake of fire. God will create a new heaven and a new earth. There will be no evil, just peace and love and joy forever. I want to be on the winning team, so I will work for the kingdom of God while I am alive on this earth and pray for forgiveness when I sin. I will take a stand for God and push back against the gates of hell. Those that are lost love their sins and try to open the gates of hell. We are in a battle. Which side are you on?

Pain

> "For we know that the whole creation groaneth and travaileth in pain together until now" (Rom. 8:22).
> "And God shall wipe away all tears from their eyes; and there shall be no more death, neither sorrow, nor crying, neither shall there be any more pain: for the former things are passed away" (Rev. 21:4).

There is much pain in this life, physical and mental. As long as the devil can roam free, mankind will experience pain. There is pain in childbirth, and pain in getting old and dying, and pain between birth and death.

There is pain that is caused by the devil that is preventable. Yes, you can avoid this type of pain if you stay on the narrow path. It is my mission to help prevent you from experiencing pain in life. You will never know how much pain you have been spared in life if you stay on the narrow path. How can you know it if it is far from you? So trust me, I know because I have experienced pain similar to what Job felt.

First of all, let me address just one of Satan's weapons: alcohol. Alcohol has been glamorized by million-dollar advertisements, and people have been brainwashed by it. Alcohol is an addictive drug and poison to the body. There are two reasons why alcoholic drinks are legal in America.

The main reason is money. Alcohol is a big multibillion-dollar business in America. The people that put money first in their lives and support the alcohol industry have sold their souls for money.

The second reason is that there is such a demand for alcohol. Why? Because it is an addictive drug! People have been brainwashed to think that alcohol is something to be desired for various reasons, none of which are true.

Now for the pain! Have you ever been to a funeral? A hospital? A morgue? How about a prison? A county jail? Have you ever woke up and didn't know where you were? Have you ever seen a dead body? Have you ever had to say good-bye forever? Did you ever kiss a loved one in a casket? Well, if not, you haven't felt the pain of the loss of a loved one that died young and died needlessly from something that could have been prevented had someone chose the narrow path.

> "Be sober, be vigilant; because your adversary the devil, as a roaring lion, walketh about, seeking whom he may devour" (1 Pet. 5:8).

Jesus, save us from the pain! Amen.

Pain

> "My heart is sore pained within me: and the terrors of death are fallen upon me" (Ps. 55:4).

There is another pain in life that is preventable. Do you know tobacco? I believe Satan gave birth to twins: alcohol and tobacco.

Years ago there were advertisements everywhere glamorizing cigarettes, another form of brainwashing to the masses. Training people to buy cigarettes so the stockholders of companies like Phillip-Morris could become wealthy. Did they care about the loss of life? No! The main drive was to make money. By the way, when they outlawed cigarette advertising in America, it happened to be at a time when they were building factories in Asia, where they were not required to even put warnings on the packs of cigarettes.

Cigarettes have nicotine in them, a drug as powerful and addictive as heroin. How many lives are destroyed by the tobacco industry? Worldwide, it has to be in the millions. Have you ever had a relative die from lung cancer? I have, and it's something I wouldn't wish on my worst enemy. Satan is the ruler of this present world; and his goal is to kill, steal, and destroy. And he has used tobacco as one of his many weapons. You see, he has an earthly army of soldiers. When Satan says, go forth and sell this or that, and I will make you rich, these are people who have sold their souls to the devil in exchange for riches. Did you ever wonder who can afford to build these large and beautiful waterfront homes? Well, think of it this way: each stone or brick represents a person addicted to tobacco or alcohol, and each home is a monument to someone who died a horrible death.

"For the love of money is the root of all evil"
(1 Tim. 6:1).

Where is the moral and ethical conviction in big business? It starts with each individual person. If you don't know Jesus Christ, chances are you are not familiar with his teachings, like love your neighbor as yourself or do unto others as you would have them do unto you.

America is Christian by name only. If she were full of real Christians, she would be full of life, not death! Wake up! Stand up! Voice an opinion! Speak up for those loved ones in their graves and say, "Enough! Stop killing us, Mr. Big Business!"

Whenever I see a major sports event, I am amazed at the turnout of enthused fans, and all that over a ball! Well, we have one that created a ball called earth—Jesus Christ. Where is the enthusiasm for the power to set us free from deception?

Jesus, you have set me free from alcohol and tobacco. Thank you, Lord Jesus, I love you! Amen.

Pain

> "The sorrows of death compassed me, and the pains of hell gat hold upon me: I found trouble and sorrow" (Ps. 116:3).

Another avoidable pain is the pain of drug addiction. There is so much pain involved in the life of the addict. First there is the physical pain of withdrawal from a substance; then the emotional pain of hopelessness; and then the pain of human degradation to the point of neglecting proper diet, cleanliness, and personal appearance. Then there is the neglect of responsibilities of paying for necessities such as food, rent, utilities, etc. But the most evil thing is the neglecting the children. A child that grows up with drug-addicted parents will bear the mental and emotional scars and the memory of it for the rest of their life.

If you are an addict, get help! There are plenty of programs available. Step out in faith. Jesus Christ can work through people to get you the help you need. All you need is faith the size of a mustard seed and you can say to that mountain, "Move," and it shall move.

There is something more painful than your withdrawal pains and that is the pain you put your family through. Drug addiction is a selfish disease. If only you knew the pain you inflict on your mother, father, siblings, and, yes, your children. I have seen the mental, physical, and emotional scars on children of drug addicts. It is all unnecessary! Don't use the excuse, "I am self-medicating due to my past emotional hurts." If you need counseling, go get it. Don't drag your children through a life of horrors due to your problems. It's not fair to the kids.

I have been to five funerals within six years, four of them were within six months of each other.

Pain is seeing your sons, daughter-in-law, and brother lying dead of drug overdoses. Pain is trying to explain to your friends what happened. Pain is looking into the tear-filled eyes of your grandchildren and watching them looking at their parents in their caskets. Pain is knowing in your heart that you will have to pay for their funerals. Pain is spending your life savings on funerals because life insurance doesn't pay off for drug overdose, if they even have any life insurance. Pain is knowing you will be spending your retirement years raising grandchildren. Yes, even though you love them dearly, it is still painful. But it has been a blessing to my personal and spiritual growth. I am so very proud of my successful grandchildren and so would their parents be if they were here to see.

So, Mr. and Mrs. Party Person, stop thinking of yourself and look at what you are doing to those around you. One more thing I need to say to the addict: If you don't know Jesus, the time to receive Him is now. Why? Because if you don't get recovery, you will die soon. So you might as well get right with God now. If you say you have no hope for God or yourself, then help your family now by giving up your kids and planning your funeral!

May God help you see! Amen.

Generational Curses

> "Thou shalt not bow down thyself unto them, nor serve them: for I the Lord thy God am a jealous God, visiting the iniquity of the fathers upon the children unto the third and fourth generation of them that hate me, And showing mercy unto thousands of them that love me and keep my commandments" (Deut. 5:9–10).

Exodus 20:4, same as above.
Who hates God? Read on!

> "No man can serve two masters: for either he will hate the one, and love the other; or else he will hold to the one, and despise the other. Ye cannot serve God and mammon" (Matt. 6:24).

Luke 6:13, same as above.

Mammon - material wealth or possessions as having a debasing influence
Iniquity -sin

These Bible verses are both repeated to show their importance. If you love riches, the Bible says you hate God. And if you hate God, then that will be a curse that will be passed down to your children, grandchildren, and great-grandchildren. You may think that is not fair, but who is man? Can man argue with God? If you know your place and honor God, then you will heed His warning and obey. A loving Father will warn his children in advance so they will not fall into sin. If you have already made money your god and you want to repent, it's not too late.

> "Jesus said unto him, 'If thou wilt be perfect, go and sell that thou hast, and give to the poor, and thou shalt have treasure in heaven: and come and follow me.' But when the young man heard that saying, he went away sorrowful: for he had great possessions. Then Jesus said to his disciples, 'Verily I say unto you, that a rich man shall hardly enter into the kingdom of heaven'" (Matt. 19:21–23)

Jesus comes down hard on the rich. What is wrong with a person being rich? I believe there are satanic forces pulling the strings behind the invisible realm that entice certain people to compromise their moral principles. That is, if they had any to begin with. Another problem that faces wealthy people is that they feel self-reliant, not needing to pray to God for their needs. And they hold themselves in high esteem while looking down on the poor with disgust. But the truth is that the rich are very insecure and are not happy. That is why many wealthy turn to drugs and sex and they think they can buy peoples love and admiration. Without God as their source, many fall into a den of despair. And hopelessness begins to drive them to commit suicide.

I pray to God to never give me more than I can handle in life. Amen.

> "And he said unto them, Take heed and beware of covetousness: for a man's life consisteth not in the abundance of the things which he possesseth" (Luke 12:15).

Be Obedient to the Law

> "Think not that I am come to destroy the law or
> the prophets: I am not come to destroy, but to
> fulfill. Whosoever therefore shall break one of the
> least commandments, and shall teach men so, he
> shall be called the least in the kingdom of heaven:
> but whosoever shall do and teach them, the same
> shall be called great in the kingdom of heaven.
> For I say unto you, that except your righteous-
> ness shall exceed the righteousness of the scribes
> and Pharisees, ye shall in no case enter into the
> kingdom of heaven" (Matt. 5:17, 19, 20).

When Jesus talks, I listen. There is no other voice of authority
that I will obey. I don't care how big your church is or how good your
pastor preaches. I have to be obedient to what Jesus says.

Yes, we are living under grace, and yes, God does forgive our
sins, and I thank God for that or I would end up in hell. But God
sent His Son to show the world mercy, grace, forgiveness, and a better way to live. So let's take what Jesus taught and add those things to
the foundation that was already there. The Ten Commandments are
not the Ten Suggestions. What was considered to be an abomination
in the Old Testament is still an abomination today.

The scribes and Pharisees had an outward appearance of holiness. They were careful to be seen by men to do everything to keep
the Law of Moses. Inwardly, they were engaging in sin in secret.

What a true Christian needs to do is keep all the commandments of Moses and go to church as an outward appearance of our
faith. But also add Jesus living inside of our hearts, cleansing our
inner being, as to not sin in secret. One without the other is to live
a lie. Without Jesus to wash the inner man is like putting on clean
clothes everyday but never taking a shower or bath. The clean clothes
only cover a dirty body.

Clean both the inner and outer man, then faith with works
will show commitment to Christ and the purified heart and mind

to show honesty, integrity, and purity. Then add the grace of God through Christ and find sanctification and victory over the flesh.

When you accept Jesus as Lord, don't take two steps forward, then stop and look back. Instead, prepare for a walk that will be a lifelong journey, never looking back. Keep moving forward toward heaven. Amen.

Homosexuality

> "Thou shalt not lie with mankind, as with womankind: it is abomination" (Lev. 18:22).

It is out of love that I write this to the homosexual. I don't want to see anyone go to hell when they die, so please don't be offended.

If you are homosexual out of pure lust, then you are controlled by a demon of lust and you need to be delivered and set free. Go to a full gospel or Pentecostal church that believes in prayer and fasting, repentance and baptism.

If you are homosexual because you feel you were born that way and you feel genuine love for your partner, then you may be under a generational curse that was passed down to you. Either way, you need to be delivered from that curse to be set free. There is hope! If you have tried to get set free from the curse of homosexuality but are still tempted, remember that you are not alone. Many heterosexuals are tempted to commit the sin of fornication and adultery, and they are called to repent from that sin. Temptation is not a sin until we act upon it. Jesus said, "If a man looks at a woman and has thoughts of lust, he has committed adultery already in his heart." So the same high standards that Jesus requires of heterosexuals applies to homosexuals. Calling yourself gay doesn't give you a free pass to engage in sex. If your pastor says it's okay, he/she is wrong. That would be the same as a pastor telling the congregation it's permissible to commit adultery and for the singles to have premarital sex. God does not have a double standard. Jesus calls for everyone to repent of their sin, and then he forgives the sin. The narrow path is a path that all Christians need to find as a path to the Father and life everlasting.

If you reject my view, well, you can go and find a church that accepts homosexuals. They will say it's okay and the pastor is gay or lesbian and you can feel a false sense of eternal security, but the outcome will be an eternity in hell. The choice is yours. I have done what Jesus wants me to do. I have warned you out of love!

I have pointed toward a way out! Remember, Satan is a liar. Jesus came to set the captive free! Amen.

> "If the Son therefore shall make you free, ye shall be free indeed" (John 8:36).

Limitations

> "And beside all this, between us and you there is a great gulf fixed: so that they which would pass from hence to you cannot; neither can they pass to us, that would come from thence" (Luke 16:26).

The above verse is referring to the location of the rich man who died and went to hell. He was in torment in the heat and flame, and he could not escape from that place. He begged to get out, but it was too late. He was limited to how far he could go. There was a limit to the area he was in.

I often think about traveling to different countries, but I am limited to what I can afford to do. If I had enough money, I could go just about anywhere in the world. What a great feeling of freedom. Just pack a bag and go somewhere, anywhere.

What about after we die? Will we be free to go anywhere? I think not. Our body will be in the grave until the resurrection. So we will exist as a soul or our conscience, whatever that is. We will be at God's mercy and judgment when we die. How do you know how much control you will have over your soul, as far as traveling or moving about in the afterlife?

God has prepared a place for those that love and serve Him. I thank God for that, and I trust God that He will send His angels to escort me to heaven someday. I put my future in God's hands, just as I trust God now in this life. By obeying God, I put limitations on my life. I am not free to do whatever I feel like. I am not free to find worldly pleasures that are sinful. By setting boundaries in my life, I can feel confident that God will reward me with more freedoms in the next life.

In this life on earth, you can be the richest, strongest, most powerful person in the world but how much control do you have over your own soul? Don't you see, your soul is subject to God's will and ultimately your future will depend on what you do for God in this life? Don't make the mistake of thinking you will be free to come and go as you please after you die. Your soul is trapped in your body while you live, so that proves your soul cannot travel at your will.

If you would heed this warning, then live to serve Jesus Christ and He will show mercy to the merciful. Ask and you shall receive. Amen.

Sex Offenders

> "But whoso shall offend one of these little ones which believe in me, it were better for him that a millstone were hanged about his neck, and that he were drowned in the depth of the sea" (Matt. 18:6)

Sex offenders and child molesters all fall under demons inhabiting the person, controlling them. This is very serious because it is something that happens even within the church.

There was a big cover-up by the Catholic Church and is still being investigated. How can this happen? The reasons are too many to list here. I want to give a message to those that are tormented by the demonic.

If you have feelings toward children, you know who you are. If you don't care about your victims and you are so far and deeply possessed, then you are going to be punished severely in this life and in the next. Jesus spoke of punishments above and beyond the scope of hellfire.

If you are truly repentant, you need to turn from every lustful demon and embrace Jesus Christ with every bit of strength in your being. You need to destroy any and all pornographic material and read your Bible daily, pray, fast, join a Bible-believing church, and be active as a Christian.

You need to refuse any ministry that would have any contact with children.

You need to understand that Jesus is forgiving to those that come to him with a repentant heart, but you must do everything in your power to turn from this sin. If you still have temptations to molest children, then it's time to seek medical help.

You need to try everything that is available to kill this evil that lives inside you. Don't underestimate the power of Satan. He comes to kill, steal, and destroy.

Satan will kill a person's conscience.

Satan will use that person to abuse and even kill.

Satan will steal the innocence of children.

Satan will destroy two lives, the victim and the abuser. Some abusers were once victims of abuse themselves. They may be victims of a generational curse.

Having exhausted all means of prevention of child abuse, the offender should offer himself up to God. I would rather read, "Man found dead from suicide" than "Child found raped and murdered."

Lord, call all to repent and protect us from all evil in Jesus's name. Amen.

Thine Heart

"Stand in awe, and sin not: commune with your own heart upon your bed, and be still. Selah" (Ps. 4:4).

"My son, forget not my law; but let thine heart keep my commandments: For length of days, and long life and peace, shall they add to thee" (Prov. 3:1, 2).

Let thine heart keep my commandments. When your heart is in something, it becomes a labor of love. You will actually enjoy keeping God's commandments. First of all, to be obedient; secondly, to reap the benefits; and thirdly, to obtain the peace of mind and security that comes with pleasing God.

> "In all thy ways acknowledge Him, and He shall direct thy paths" (Prov. 3:6).

Don't be afraid to acknowledge Jesus; it is also necessary that we do.

> "But whosoever shall deny me before men, him will I also deny before my father which is in heaven" (Matt. 10:33).

We can be guilty of denying Christ before men by our actions. The world of lost souls can be our worst judge. Why? They know more scriptures than you may think. So if you tell the world you are a Christian, they will judge your actions. If you are living in sin, you deny Christ by your actions. Peter denied Christ three times, then he wept bitterly and repented. Help us, Lord, to live a life that is worthy of our calling. Amen.

God's Grace

> "Wherefore we receiving a kingdom which cannot be moved, let us have grace, whereby we may serve God acceptably with reverence and Godly fear: For our God is a consuming fire" (Heb. 12:28, 29).

We are saved by God's grace, we are sustained by God's grace, and we need God's grace every day to keep us going.

It is God's grace that forgives and picks us up when we stumble and fall. We need to press forward all the more to seek correction for our soul. There is none worthy of redemption, only God's grace can see us through to another day.

"And the child grew, and waxed strong in spirit, filled with wisdom: and the grace of God was upon him" (Luke 2:40).

"Now to him that worketh is the reward not reckoned of grace, but of debt" (Rom. 4:4).

"My son, hear the instruction of thy father, and forsake not the law of thy mother: For they shall be an ornament of grace unto thy head, and chains about thy neck" (Prov. 1:8, 9).

"For the law was given by Moses, but grace and truth came by Jesus Christ" (John 1:17).

School Teachers

"Specially the day that thou stoodest before the Lord thy God in Horeb, when the Lord said unto me, gather me the people together and I will make them hear my words, that they may learn to fear me all the days that they shall live upon the earth, and that they may teach their children" (Deut. 4:10)

It's time to change the policies in the public schools. There are many public school teachers that are good teachers and love the children. It is a shame that they were victims of a liberal left- wing-controlled college system that required them to bow down to false gods of humanistic, Antichrist teachings. Not only Antichrist, but they were taught to accept homosexuals as normal and godliness as something to look down on as being outdated and unacceptable with the modern method of teaching.

I call on all you good teachers that have faith in Jesus Christ to bring God back to the public schools. Do not think it can't be done. Put a godly symbol on your vehicles to show your support for bringing God back, to bless the schools again. A fish symbol or a cross will do. As you see your numbers increase, your faith will grow.

We can change our country and the world. Stand up and be counted. Let's bring prayer back to school.

America is the land of the free. Why can't the children have the freedom to be taught the basics of the Christian religion in public schools?

> "In like manner also, that women adorn themselves in modest apparel, with shamefacedness and sobriety; not with braided hair, or gold, or pearls, or costly array" (1 Tim. 2:9).

It is right to cover yourself and to dress modestly. Outward beauty can be deceptive. It is the inner beauty that attracts the godly man, and the godly man will love you for who you are as a person. It is right to be kind, helpful, polite, modest, humble, and willing to serve others. It is right to be truthful, honest, trustworthy, dependable, loyal, reverent, and brave. It is right to share, instruct, and stand up for what is right. It is right to fight for the weak, the downtrodden, the helpless, the mentally challenged, and the disabled. It is right to lend an ear to the lost, broken, rejected, and brokenhearted.

It is right to find forgiveness in your heart, to be kind and gentle. It is right to exercise, to build, to create, to have hobbies, to paint, to draw, to travel, to have adventures. It is right to learn, to read, to study, and to teach others. It is right to eat healthy, in moderation, and take care of yourself. It is right to enjoy life, to live life, to laugh, and to be happy and full of joy. It is right to take on responsibilities, to work hard, to do a good job, and to take pride in your work.

It is right to pray before each meal and thank God for everything. It is right to use your time wisely, not to be wasteful, but to be thrifty. It is right to save some money for a rainy day. You don't know what the future may bring. It is right to be generous and charitable, to share your food, to lend but not to borrow unnecessarily. It is right to ask God for whatever you need, but don't be greedy for gain. It is right to repent of sin but also, as God forgives, you must also forgive. It is right to forgive yourself, live and learn. Don't repeat your mistakes.

Love God, people, and love yourself. Amen.

What Follows You?

> "Surely goodness and mercy shall follow me all the days of my life: and I will dwell in the house of the Lord forever" (Ps. 23:6).
>
> "And did all drink the same spiritual drink: for they drank of that spiritual Rock that followed them: and that Rock was Christ. But with many of them God was not well pleased: for they were overthrown in the wilderness. Now these things were our examples, to the intent we should not lust after evil things, as they also lusted. Neither let us commit fornication, as some of them committed, and fell in one day, thee and twenty thousand" (1 Cor. 10:4, 5, 6, 8).

There is no hope for those that reject Christ! Even those that were considered to be God's chosen people. They followed Moses out of Egypt and were delivered by God. They ate the manna from heaven, and they drank from the spiritual Rock that was Christ. In one day, twenty-three thousand died. Why? Because they fell into sin. They lusted after evil. If God didn't spare them, he will not spare us either. It is by prayer and reading the Bible that we are strong enough to resist the devil, so pray every day and take God's warnings seriously.

Warning Signs

God speaks to us in many ways: the inner voice, our conscience, guilt feelings, our pastors, our elders, our parents, our teachers, the Bible, our leaders, and our laws. But what happens when evil corrupts our nation and the leaders become corrupt and they change the laws to accept evil, when our teachers are brainwashed by corrupt college professors that hold up their many diplomas and degrees as to say in their heart, "I have ascended higher than God in my learning." Like Lucifer, they have fallen from grace to a level lower than a primitive life form, corrupted and going forth to teach corruption. They no longer try to hide from the face of God. They parade with a banner of pride and celebrate their fallen state of debauchery. These are men and women that are no longer connected to the things of God but require the praises of men. Our Ivy League universities need to repent and go back to the basics that they were built upon, many which were started as Bible-based colleges.

Jesus Christ is a personal savior, but one by one we have lost our way and are in need of a good shepherd to lead us back into the fold. I have experienced much hardship and grief in my life, but I claim the promises of Psalm 23:6, "Goodness and mercy shall follow me all the days of my life, and I will dwell in the house of the Lord forever. Amen."

Get to Know God

"For I desired mercy and not sacrifice; and the knowledge of God more than burnt offerings" (Hos. 6:6).

To know God is to receive peace. To know Jesus is to show mercy. To receive the knowledge of God is to die to sin and self and to receive a vision of God's holiness.

Oil and water do not mix. Like sin and holiness, they war against each other within the spirit. There is no truce, only victory or defeat. When sin is victorious, then we feel defeated. When holiness has its way, then the heart is pure and peace will reside in that soul. God will be with you in the night and strengthen you when you are feeling forsaken and unsure. God is always within reach. All we have to do is reach out to God, and He will help us in our struggles in life.

Separate yourselves from the evil of this world. Look at the beauty of God's creation and know that God is great—the mountains, the rivers, the blue sky, and white fluffy clouds. Feel the warmth of the sun. May it light up your soul.

Look at the beauty of the animals. Look at how the mothers take care of their young. They pick up their pups with sharp teeth, gently, careful not to hurt, and yet ready to fight to protect them. God prepared nature in a most wonderful way. There is a time and a season for everything in life.

Repent and return to common sense of nature and see the error of your ways. Pray that the Lord of hosts will be merciful and call you as a lost sheep when you are found by the shepherd.

One day at a time, one step at a time, always moving forward to the holiness of God.

Thank you, Lord God, for your wonderful creation! Amen.

God's Warning of Judgment

> "And I heard another voice from heaven, saying, Come out of her, my people that ye be not partakers of her sins, and that ye receive not of her plagues. For her sins have reached unto heaven and God hath remembered her iniquities. Reward her even as she rewarded you, and double unto her double according to her works: in the cup which she hath filled fill to her double" (Rev. 18:4–6).

"Come out of her my people" was a voice from heaven, heard by the apostle John. This is definitely a warning from God to His people, Christians. This warning refers to Babylon the Great. Babylon could be a reference to any city or center of luxurious, sinful life.

I fear for America. Why? As a Right to Life supporter, I receive information as to the status of abortions in America. As of this writing, there have been sixty-three million abortions performed. If America is Babylon and God is going to double His judgment, then over one hundred million will die. If that is God's will, then so be it. The important part is to not be partakers of her sins. To leave the country would be impossible for most, so to come out of her would mean to prepare yourself spiritually to not be a part of the sinful nature of the sinfulness that has permeated society. Remember Lot. He lived in Sodom, but he didn't take part in their sinfulness. And because of his righteousness, God sent two angels to save Lot and his family from destruction. I believe God will save the righteous Christians by taking us out of the world at the Rapture of the Church. Amen.

The Rapture of the Church

The Church is the body of Christ that is made up of all truly born-again Christians from all nations around the world, from all diverse Christian religions. The Church does not mean any one denomination. If you are in a sect that claims to be the only one that is right, you are being taught wrongly and are in a cult. You need to read your Bible and seek the Lord's wisdom, to get out of that cult, and find a good church where you will be taught the truth with love.

> "Now this I say, brethren, that flesh and blood cannot inherit the kingdom of God; neither doth corruption inherit incorruption. Behold, I show you a mystery; We shall not all sleep, but we shall all be changed. In a moment, in the twinkling of an eye, at the last trump: for the trumpet shall sound, and the dead shall be raised incorruptible, and we shall be changed" (1 Cor. 15:50, 51, 52).

Now is the time to prepare yourself spiritually to be ready to meet the Lord. For not all that call themselves Christian will be taken up in the Rapture. Do not be misled. Jesus said He would return like a thief in the night, when we least expect it. There are twenty-four hours in a day. We must be ready at every minute of the day or night. I have heard a preacher say Jesus has forgiven all our sins, past, present, and future. Do not be fooled. I say Jesus has forgiven our past sins that we have truly repented from. But if we are presently sinning, then that means we have not repented yet. And as far as the future, no one knows the future, only God. So be careful of false teachers. They lead many down the wrong path. We are living in the last days; the Rapture can happen at any time.

> "For the Lord himself shall descend from heaven with a shout, with the voice of the archangel, and with the trump of God: and the dead in Christ shall rise first: 17- Then we which are alive and remain shall be caught up together with them in the clouds, to meet the Lord in the air: and so shall we ever be with the Lord" (1 Thess. 4:16, 17).

The word *rapture* means to be snatched up or caught up. Be ready at all times. Repent. Turn away from all sin. Do not be misled by the false teaching of once saved always saved. God said, "I will not be mocked." Do you think that at the moment the Rapture happens that the Lord will take you up to heaven if you are watching porn or engaging in adultery or fornication? Don't be dumb. The most illiterate person can understand this, as long as they have the Holy Spirit. You can't measure a person's spirituality by their level of academic achievements. The apostles were uneducated men, yet they are held in the highest esteem and honor in all the Christian churches because they were filled with the Holy Spirit.

If you believe in Christ and you miss the Rapture, then you will have to live through the Tribulation. That's the bad news. The good news is you can still be saved, but it may cost you your life. Whatever happens, *do not* accept the mark of the beast or you will be damned for eternity.

Lord Jesus, give us wisdom. Amen.

The Mark of the Beast

> "And he causeth all, both small and great, rich and poor, free and bond, to receive a mark in their right hand or in their foreheads" (Rev. 13:16).

What is interesting in this verse is it is a prophesy of a time in the future when people will be forced to receive a mark: *in*, not on, the hand or forehead. That tells me "the mark" will be an implanted device. The fact that this prophesy was given two thousand years ago, the technology was not available until just a few years ago. As of this writing in 2018, they are implanting microchips in animals and some people are volunteering to be implanted at work. As for the reason for implanting the forehead, this may be due to enhanced security measures and ease of scanning. The number 666 could be an ID number consisting of eighteen numbers or a combination of numbers symbols and letters. As six plus six plus six equals eighteen. Whatever the mark of the beast is, *do not* receive it! I believe this is going to be a form of identification that will utilize the most modern technology and will be connected to the World Wide Web. WWW = 666.

In the Hebrew, text letters had a numerical value and the W = 6.

> "And that no man might buy or sell, save he that had the mark, or the name of the beast, or the number of his name. Here is wisdom, Let him that hath understanding count the number of the beast: for it is the number of a man; and his number is Six hundred three score and six" (Rev. 13:17–18).

This form of identification will be forced on the whole world, first by economic pressure and eventually by penalty of death to all that refuse the mark. Those that receive the mark of the beast will also be required to worship the beast, which will be a world leader. This world leader will come in the name of peace but will be the devil in the flesh. He will be a counterfeit form of Christ, the Antichrist, and will deceive many. That is why it is of utmost importance to study the Word of God so you will not be fooled.

> "And he had power to give life unto the image of the beast, that the image of the beast shall both speak, and cause that as many as would not worship the image of the beast should be killed" (Rev. 13:15).

I believe that the "Beast" is a name of something that the apostle John saw in the vision of the future trying to describe a computer. And "the Image that speaks" is AI (artificial intelligence) speaking through an (image) or a hologram of a personage of a false God that offers mankind the solution to world problems but in reality will enslave mankind.

> "And I saw thrones, and they sat upon them, and judgment was given unto them: *and I saw the souls of them that were beheaded for the witness of Jesus and for the word of God,* and which had not worshipped the beast, neither his image, neither had received his mark upon their foreheads, or in their hands; and they lived and reigned with Christ a thousand years" (Rev. 20:4).

Born Again

> "Jesus answered and said unto him, Verily, verily, I say unto thee, except a man be born again, he cannot see the kingdom of God" (John 3:3).
> "Jesus answered, 'Verily, verily, I say unto thee, except a man be born of water and of the Spirit, he cannot enter into the kingdom of God" (John 3:5).

You have church attendees and you have born-again Christians. The church's mainline denominations such as Catholics, Methodists, etc. believe in the church. The born-again churches like Baptists, Assemblies of God, etc. believe you must make Christ the ruler of your heart and life.

When you are born a baby into this world, you are physically born. When you accept Jesus Christ into your heart and are baptized in His name, you are born of water and Spirit. You become a new creation, a new creature. There is no way to fully comprehend what happens in the spiritual realm because you are a baby in Christ when you become born again. You will feel different. A good church will feed the new Christian babes the milk of the word, and as you mature in Christ, you will get the meat and potatoes of the Word. The sad thing is a lot of born-again Christians remain babes in Christ, never developing to their full potential.

It is the work of Satan to try to destroy the churches, and he has done a lot of damage. His methodology is to cause division. Church doctrine has divided churches and people within the Christian faith for centuries. Christians from different faiths have fought and killed each other over their differences.

There is only one Jesus Christ, yet so many different Christian churches. There is really no excuse today for someone not to find a church where they feel comfortable. The selection is like going into a candy store to pick out a piece of candy. So many choices. The question is, do you want to feel comfortable or do you want to hear the Word of God? Sometimes the Word of God will cut you like a sharp two-edged sword. Are you brave enough to come out of your comfort zone?

When Jesus returns, there will be no more divisions by church denominations. The churches that teach and preach the words of Christ will receive the greater reward when Jesus returns. At that time, there will be no more churches, only the body of Christ, a body of believers, all united, with one mind, one spirit. You become a member of the body of Christ when you become a born-again Christian. Amen.

Blessings

"The blessing of the Lord, it maketh rich, and he addeth no sorrow with it" (Prov. 10:22).
"And I am sure that, when I come unto you, I shall come in the fullness of the blessing of the gospel of Christ" (Rom. 15:29).

Jesus died for all but not all received salvation, and those that have salvation, not all have received blessings. Seek and find, ask and receive, knock and the door will be opened.

Put Jesus in your heart, soul, and mind; and put God first and all things will work together for the good in your life.

Put God last on your list of priorities, and you will always wonder why you are not blessed. If you plant an apple tree, don't expect to pick oranges.

> "Sow to yourselves in righteousness, reap in mercy; break up your fallow ground: for it is time to seek the Lord, till He come and rain righteousness upon you" (Hos. 10:12).

Do you want God's blessings? Then seek God and His kingdom, and move Jesus to the top of your list of priorities. All it takes is the faith of a child, not a PhD. It is so simple, yet to the spiritually blind, it is like walking on water. The Bible is foolishness to those that are perishing. They become slaves to their own sins and not willing to bend their knees to God. They stand tall and proud as they slowly sink in the mire of eternal damnation, laughing and scoffing at everything that is holy.

Lord, open the eyes and touch the hearts of everyone that reads these words. Amen.

The Unpardonable Sin

> "Wherefore I say unto you, All manner of sin and blasphemy shall be forgiven unto men: but the blasphemy against the Holy Ghost shall not be forgiven unto men" (Matt. 12:31).

Jesus said this after the Pharisees accused Him of obtaining power from the devil to be able to heal a man that was possessed with a devil, blind, and dumb.

The Holy Spirit can only empower Christians. And Christians that are filled with the Holy Spirit can only do the will of God when being directed by the Holy Spirit. The outcome can only be good, as in helping people and meeting their needs.

Anyone that condemns a Christian as being from the devil is committing the unpardonable sin. That only applies to the Christian that is doing the will of God and has the Holy Spirit. For example, in the book *Foxes Book of Martyrs*, the church of Rome tortured and killed many Protestants by order from the pope, all because they believed in the Word of God from the Bible. The fact is they were persecuted because they were led by the Holy Spirit. When the Catholic Church felt threatened by the people of the Reformation started by Martin Luther, they committed some of the most barbaric forms of torture imaginable. So how can one religion persecute another with all the cruelty of the powers of hell? To call good evil, and evil good must be the unpardonable sin and blasphemy against the Holy Spirit, for as Jesus commands us to love our enemies, we should be able to agree to disagree in peace.

Another way to commit the unpardonable sin is to reject Jesus Christ as your personal Lord and Savior. That is the ultimate sin from which there is no forgiveness from because there would be no remedy. After all, Jesus was filled with the Holy Spirit and to reject Jesus is to reject the Holy Spirit.

We need to pray for wisdom and discernment in order to sense the Holy Spirit. An outward symbol can be misleading. Just because a person wears a cross around their neck doesn't make them a Christian. Just like wearing a New York Yankee's ball cap doesn't make them a major league baseball player.

Prosperity Preachers

> "Perverse disputing of men of corrupt minds, and destitute of the truth, supposing that gain is godliness; from such withdraw thyself" (1 Tim. 6:5).

Be careful not to be deceived by men that entice you with words concerning prosperity. They have a message that is basic and devoid of the spiritual truth of God. Their goal is for their own personal gain. They measure wealth and compare that with measuring God's blessings. Their main message is the more money you have or the more material things you have means the more you are blessed by God.

This is false teaching, plain and simple. As a matter of fact, Jesus tells us to be content with having the basics in life and that a man's life does not consist of how much he has materially. It is harder for a rich man to enter into heaven, almost impossible, if not for God's grace. So knowing this, why would a Christian even want to be rich? Riches are a trap and a snare.

Give generously to your church and remember those less fortunate. Be charitable, and God will reward you. Give and it shall be given, but don't give to get! That is a wrong motive. It's called greed. Repent of greed and seek spiritual blessings. Amen.

Do Not Be Deceived

> "Let no man deceive you with vain words: for because of these things cometh the wrath of God upon the children of disobedience. Be not ye therefore partakers with them" (Eph. 5:6, 7).

The true Christian walk is quite plain and straightforward. It is so simplistic that a child can understand it, yet a PhD in theology could become so laden down with vain babblings that they will talk themselves into a hellish nightmare, devoid of the Holy Spirit. We must learn to separate our spirit from our intellect and fill our spirit with the wisdom of God to be able to discern between right and wrong. If you try to rationalize why your flesh wants to war against your spirit, you will give in to accepting sin as being nonexistent. At that point you will make your intellect be your god.

Lay your soul before God, and repent from your sins. Prepare to receive the baptism of the Holy Ghost and receive the cleansing power of Jesus Christ, the sacrificial Lamb that has the power to forgive sins.

Stand up and be renewed in spirit. Count yourself worthy to be called a child of God. Turn your back on all evil and walk toward the light of Jesus. Be baptized in "the name of the Father, the Son, And the Holy Spirit," Amen.

You have an enemy, the devil, and you are fighting in a war. So choose your friends carefully. The best friend you could choose is Jesus Christ.

Society will pass laws to allow sin to be acceptable behavior. When this happens, God's wrath will be against that nation because they have turned off the inner voice that convicts them when they sin. It is at that point where they will be given over to a reprobate mind, no longer able to discern between good and evil, no longer able to make good decisions. They will be turned into hell, and they will not be able to escape judgment. They will follow after an evil leader and will lose all natural love and affection toward the things of God. They will despise all godly authority and will be rebellious in nature.

There is coming a great gathering and separation. Those that love evil and lawlessness on the left and those that love God and the law on the right. Then there will be peace on earth for one thousand years. Then after the one thousand years, Satan will be unchained to temp mankind with evil one more time. After this time of testing, Satan will be cast into the lake of fire. Amen.

Persecuted, Not Forsaken

> "And he went out to meet Asa, and said unto him, Hear ye me, Asa, and all Judah, and Benjamin; The Lord is with you, while ye be with him; and if ye seek him, he will be found of you; but if ye forsake him, He will forsake you" (2 Chron. 15:2).
>
> "Let your conversation be without covetousness; and be content with such things as ye have: for he hath said, I will never leave thee, nor forsake thee" (Heb. 13:5).
>
> "Persecuted, but not forsaken, cast down, but not destroyed" (2 Cor. 4:9).

Sometimes we feel forsaken by God, but as long as we stay on the narrow path, we can be sure that God is with us every step of the way. Even when things are going wrong and there is death all around us, keep your eyes on God and Jesus Christ and know without a doubt that God is with you. Examine yourself and turn from every sin in your life. Destroy any idols you have hidden away. Remember God's warning to Asa and all Judah: "If you forsake me, I will forsake you."

Israel had fallen into idol worship, and because they did, they had no peace but great vexation for God did vex them with all adversity. When Asa turned back to God and destroyed the abominable idols, he then entered into a covenant to seek God with all their heart and soul. He even removed his mother, the queen, from her throne, because she had made an idol.

An idol can be a statue that you pray to or a stronghold in your life that you refuse to give up. Anything that is stronger than or replaces God's perfect will for your life. It can be alcohol, drugs, sex, money, power, anger, lies, materialism, witchcraft, work, sports, gossip, video games, etc., anything that controls or elevates itself to the status of an idol or false god.

Make room in your heart for a golden throne and put Jesus on that throne. If you put Jesus first in your life, you can be assured that He will never leave you or forsake you.

Even when family and friends turn against you, Jesus will be with you. Make wise and godly choices in this life, and you will be rewarded in this life and in heaven. Amen.

Submit and Resist

> "Submit yourselves therefore to God. Resist the devil and he will flee from you" (James 4:7).

When you are tempted by the devil, you must resist. But to be victorious over the devil it takes more than to just resist him and then go on your way. To be victorious over the devil, you must submit to God.

When you are tempted to sin, pray to God in submission first and ask God what you should do? Be humble with a servant's attitude. By putting God first, you will gain extra power to resist the devil. However, if you leave out God and put all your focus on the devil, then you are operating on your own strength. Man is no match for Satan and his demons.

That is why many times people with addictions try and fail over and over and many give up hope. They try to beat the devil without God. For some reason they get angry with God for the situation they put themselves in. Therefore, not being able to receive the very power they need to resist the devil.

This is not a game. This is life and death. Freedom vs. slavery. Before you resist the devil, submit yourselves to God. Amen.

Do Not Tempt Others

> "It is good neither to eat flesh nor to drink wine, nor anything whereby thy brother stumbleth, or is offended, or is made weak. Hast thou faith? Have it to thyself before God. Happy is he that condemneth not himself in that thing which he alloweth" (Rom. 14:21, 22).

Many Christians believe in abstaining from drinking alcoholic beverages. To some it is sinful; to others they are in recovery. Whatever the reason, we should respect other people's choices in that matter. If a person can have one or two drinks and not be affected by the alcohol, then to that person I suppose it's not a sin. But that person should not drink in front of a brother or sister in the Lord, especially if they know that the other person has a problem with alcohol. The same goes for eating certain meats or foods that a brother or sister in the Lord finds offensive or sinful.

The Bible is clear in stating that it is sin to get drunk. The Bible says a drunkard will not enter the Kingdom of God, so why take the chance of becoming a drunkard by tempting yourself and others to drink? The law states that if you drink more than two drinks and drive, you are impaired. Over .1 percent alcohol in your blood and you are legally drunk. Not only are you a danger on the road, your judgment is impaired so much that you could lower your moral standards to the point of allowing yourself to commit immoral acts of sin. When this happens, the devil will take advantage of the situation, and temptation will cause many to fall.

I have found that total abstinence from alcohol is what is best for me. I have seen alcohol ruin lives and lead people into other drugs. I have seen people that seem to have their drinking under control, only to find out that they were caught driving drunk.

So be warned. Alcohol is a tool of Satan. When Jesus turned the water into wine, it was nonalcoholic wine. Why would Jesus tempt people to get drunk? Jesus never sinned. I believe that if Jesus did drink a glass of wine with alcohol in it, he wouldn't have sinned because he would only have one glass.

Remember this, Jesus was in control over every aspect of His flesh while he walked the earth. Thank you, Jesus, for being the perfect example. Jesus came to earth to be our savior because that is what everyone needs. Man cannot save himself. Amen.

God Is Not Blind to Sin

> "But know that the Lord hath set apart him that is godly for Himself: the Lord will hear when I call unto Him. Stand in awe, and sin not: commune with your own heart upon your bed, and be still. Selah" (Ps. 4:3, 4).
>
> "The foolish shall not stand in thy sight: thou hatest all workers of iniquity. For thou, Lord, wilt bless the righteous; with favor wilt thou compass him as with a shield" (Ps. 5:5, 12).
>
> "God judgeth the righteous, and God is angry with the wicked every day" (Ps. 7:11).

Synonyms for *wicked*: sinful, criminal, guilty, unjust, unrighteous, unholy, irreligious, ungodly, profane, vicious, atrocious, nefarious, heinous, flagrant, flagitious, abandoned (Webster's Dictionary)

To repent of a certain sin is to turn away from that sin and go in the opposite direction. To turn your back on that sin is to hate and detest and renounce that sin. In doing so, you can call on the Lord to forgive and to strengthen your resolve to be free from the bondage of the sin.

To say in your heart I am drowning in my sins and I am too weak to have victory over my sins and think that the Lord will save you in that condition is to be a lazy and wicked person.

There is no sin too strong or too big for God. Why do you think Jesus died on the cross? If it was okay to continue to live in sin, then His death was in vain. That would mean that His death on the cross accomplished nothing! No way! Jesus overcame death and hell and the grave. He resurrected himself in great power over evil. When we walk with Jesus down the narrow path He referred to, we do not walk alone. Jesus is with us and gives us the power of the Holy Spirit.

Yes, we will have our struggles and some battles are easier than others, but the battle against evil is the Lord's.

So put on the whole armor of Christ and battle against sin in your life with the battle cry, "I can do all things with Jesus Christ, who strengthens me."

Stand up and fight against the sin that tries to hold you back from achieving what God has purposed for your life! Amen.

All Temptation Is Evil

> "Let no man say when he is tempted, I am tempted of God: For God cannot be tempted with evil, neither tempted He any man" (James 1:13).

It is important to realize that all temptation comes from the devil. Knowing that will prepare your mind and spirit for a battle.

One of the most frustrating parts of war is not being able to identify the enemy. The more we study God's Word by reading the Bible, the more we are given the wisdom to identify the enemy.

As we examine ourselves, our motives, our desires, we need to ask the question, where did that thought come from or what was I thinking? If you don't have a good feeling about something, or if you are uncomfortable about a purchase or a friendship, you need to pray to God for some answers. You also need to check the Word of God and use it as a guide.

It is not God that tempts us; it is the devil. And a dangerous sin is pride. Oftentimes a Christian that has achieved significant levels of success in life will become prideful. When that happens, they have set themselves up to be tempted by the devil. And God will allow Satan to tempt as a test and also to teach that person a lesson in humility. It is important to give God the glory for our success and to humble ourselves.

> "A man's pride shall bring him low: but honour shall uphold the humble in spirit" (Prov. 29:23).
> "For whosoever exalteth himself shall be abased; and he that humbles himself shall be exalted" (Luke 14:11)

Identify the enemy and prepare to do battle. With God's help you can be victorious. Remember, your life and your soul is at stake. Amen.

Mutual Love and Respect

> "For after this manner in the old time the holy women also, who trusted in God, adorned them-selves, being in subjection unto their own hus-bands. Even as Sara obeyed Abraham, calling him Lord: whose daughters ye are, as long as ye do well, and are not afraid with any amazement. Likewise ye husbands, dwell with them accord-ing to knowledge, giving honor unto the wife, as unto the weaker vessel, and as being heirs together of the grace of life; that your prayers be not hindered" (1 Pet 3:5–7)

There are too many single moms raising children, and my heart goes out to them. When I met my wife of twenty-eight years, she was a single mom. She worked full time and raised two children and was an active churchgoing, Bible-believing, born-again Christian. Now we are raising two grandchildren. Raising children is not an easy road. I know because I had raised four children from a previous marriage. My point in mentioning this is that in 1 Peter 3:5, he is referring to the old times. Keep in mind that this was written two thousand years ago and he is looking back to the old times. As for me, I think of the 1800s or the 1700s as the old times. I can only imagine what people were like three or four thousand years ago when the Bible says some people lived to be five hundred to nine hundred years old.

What America needs to survive is for the young people to lay hold of a vision of what a godly family was like in the old times. How about a farmer, hunter, soldier as the man of the house, who had muscles of steel from working the land to provide for his family? A man that went to church on Sunday and was ready to fight the British for independence and freedom from tyranny. A man that was willing to fight and die for a godly cause. The Revolutionary War was a fight for freedom and independence. The Civil War was a fight for freedom for the black slaves and to unite the States under one flag and the rule of law.

And the wife who also worked side by side with her husband when she wasn't busy raising the children. Times were tough, and many died young. I know because my grandmother died giving birth and my mother was raised by an aunt on another farm. People had it rough in the old days, and children respected their parents and grandparents. Society held people accountable and people earned respect by the way they lived. My mother went to school in a one-room schoolhouse where there was one teacher that taught a class comprised of students of all ages.

If you could go back in time and bring someone from the past, to see what is on television today, they would be horrified. America, wake up! This is not entertainment; this is brainwashing this generation into welcoming Satan and hell into our lives. It is time for a spiritual awakening. Lord, lead us back to purity and a simple way to live without being distracted by the technology that they say will free us but is really enslaving us. Amen.

Clean House

> "And if thy right eye offend thee, pluck it out, and cast it from thee: for it is profitable for thee that one of thy members should perish, and not that thy whole body should be cast into hell" (Matt. 5:29).

What do you have that offends you? Did you ever go to see a movie and were so offended that you got up and walked out? Have we been so conditioned to evil that nothing causes us to feel disgusted anymore. Can we watch and listen to filth and not be affected anymore?

> "Now the Spirit speaketh expressly, that in the latter times some shall depart from the faith, giving heed to seducing spirits, and doctrines of devils; speaking lies in hypocrisy; having their conscience seared with a hot iron" (1 Tim. 4:1–2).

It is much easier to clean house and get rid of things that are offensive than it would be to pluck out an eye. We are so blessed to be able to have options.

Years ago I could watch just about any movie, but today I am very selective. I probably threw in the trash over twenty-five DVDs that I owned, and the Lord convicted me that I should repent. It is important to monitor carefully what we see. There have been some very good movies made that have a wicked message or hidden agenda somewhere in them. This is another form of brainwashing, mind control, reshaping society to be something that is ungodly. Even the television shows of the 1950s and 1960s were full of drinking and smoking.

Does society shape television and movies, or does television and movies shape society? Is technology being used to brainwash a nation to be subservient to evil powers?

Lord Jesus, free us and renew our minds! Amen.

Jesus's Helpers

> "He is not here, but is risen: remember how He spake unto you when He was yet in Galilee, Saying, the Son of man must be delivered into the hands of sinful men, and be crucified, and the third day rise again. And they remembered His words" (Luke 24:6–8).

Here we have the two angels at Christ's tomb reminding Mary Magdalene and Joanna and Mary the mother of James what Jesus said when He was in Galilee.

When life gets complicated, and we become perplexed and confused as to what is happening in the world, we need to open our Bibles and read what Jesus said two thousand years ago. We can have peace then, knowing that Jesus told us everything that we need to know.

I believe we have angels to remind us and comfort us. These angels are remarkable beings. Here we have a situation where they quote word for word what Jesus had said to His followers, as it is written in the gospel of Luke, even as it was first recorded and before it was finished. Just like they were there, recording everything that Jesus said. I believe these angels were with Jesus, everywhere He went, remembering or recording everything into the heavenly archives.

What is it that your angels are recording? The Bible tells us there are books of remembrance that will be opened on Judgment Day. What will be written in your book?

I thank God for giving His son, Jesus Christ. I believe that my book of remembrance will be divided into two sections: section 1 will be BC (Before Christ) and section 2 is BA (Born Again), after receiving Christ as Savior. The good news is the first section, BC, will be blank pages because all sin before Christ has been forgotten by God. Not that God is forgetful but because He is God. He can choose to forget our sins.

Now section 2 in my book of remembrance would be my life after receiving Christ, AC. There are some sins that I have repented of and some habits I have had total victory over, thanks to the power of Christ and the angels that are my helpers. On Judgment Day, I will be glad I found the narrow path in life. But the main theme of section 2 will be how I have a testimony that I have been washed by the blood of Jesus and sanctified and saved by grace through faith. Thank you, Jesus. Amen.

Born Again to Good Works

As you read the four gospels in the New Testament, you will notice that Jesus gives us examples and parables of how we should act and what we should do. Jesus was a doer and teacher by His own example. As followers of Christ, we are to imitate His behavior and strive to be more like Him.

> "After that he poureth water into a bason, and began to wash the disciples' feet, and to wipe them with the towel wherewith he was girded" (John 13:5).

When Christ died on the cross, He opened the door for us to be born again. Jesus paid the price for our sins to be forgiven. Without Christ, there is no hope. That is why the Bible says that man cannot save himself by good works alone.

Born again is not just a mental exercise or a spiritual feeling. It is a gradual transformation of the spirit, mind, and body. Our attitude needs to change. We need to take control of our own fleshly desires rather than letting them control us.

Jesus gave us examples of people that did not make it to heaven. In these examples of failure, we find that they were rich; greedy; self-serving; lacking compassion for the poor, the sick, and the imprisoned.

These examples of failures were people that lived for their own pleasure, unrepentant. There was one example of a professing Christian that had cast out demons in Jesus's name, but Jesus said, "I do not know you."

A true Christian is active in good works. Jesus said that good works are expected by His servants.

> "If any man serve me, let him follow me; and where I am, there shall also my servant be: if any man serve me, him will my Father honour" (John 12:26).

Get your house in order. Practice your good works on those in your own family before you are ready to move out into the community. Jesus has called us to live in peace and love. Amen.

Romans Road

There are many Bible verses in the book of Romans that show us that all have sinned and that we are saved by God's grace, not by our works. This is an important basis of the Christian belief. We cannot save ourselves by our own good works. If we could, then we would not need Jesus Christ.

There is another aspect to this way of thinking, and that is, when we believe in the saving grace of Jesus Christ, we can be confident that our sins are forgiven. This is extremely important in the life of the Christian, especially the new converts or newly saved. It is guilt over past sins that tend to hold back or stifle the Christian from moving ahead with Christ to live a better life.

The whole idea of a person repenting and then expecting a new life or the concept of being born again is for that person to feel forgiven and getting another chance at life. The slate has been wiped clean, and the person can feel a newness with Jesus as Lord of their life.

The whole concept of being born again is to feel spiritually alive to the things of God, to feel connected to God, to feel a part of the family of God, and to be adopted into the body of Christ. Like sons and daughters of God, we are forgiven over and over every time we sin and ask for forgiveness. Jesus knows our weaknesses, and He will help us overcome those areas in our lives where we fail to live up to the high standards of holiness.

No two people are the same in this world. Only God knows the hardships that many people have experienced in their lives. That is why Jesus said not to judge, unless you want to be judged.

The Christian walk is a progression from the time we accepted Jesus Christ until the day we die. How far a person progresses depends on many factors. Only God is qualified to pass judgment on the individual because only God knows that person's heart. Only God knows if that person was really sorry for their sins.

Remember that once you have received the Holy Spirit, you have received a part of God's holiness and that will convict you of your sins. It is up to you to turn away from sin. This is what God wants us to do. If we become lazy and say to ourselves, "I can sin over and over and God will forgive me, so why should I worry or change my ways?" That is a very dangerous place to be. You could lose your salvation! Amen.

Blood of the Prophets

> "Then Herod, when he saw that he was mocked of the wise men, was exceeding wroth, and sent forth, and slew all the children that were in Bethlehem, and in all the coasts thereof from two years old and under, according to the time which he diligently enquired of the wise men" (Matt 2:16).
>
> "And in her was found the blood of prophets, and of saints, and of all that were slain upon the earth" (Rev. 18:24).

Satan wanted to kill Jesus, but a warning came to Joseph in a dream to take the baby Jesus and flee to Egypt. Satan gave Herod the idea to kill all the babies from two years old and under. Had Herod been told about the coming of Jesus before Jesus was born, then Herod would have had all the women that were expecting killed. Fast-forward to today's technology and Herod would have ordered all pregnant women to report to Planned Parenthood. Everyone that is a strong believer in Christ to the point that they will lead many souls from darkness into light will be and have been targeted by Satan.

> "And no marvel; for Satan himself is transformed into an angel of light" (2 Cor. 11:14).

Herod's answer to not being able to find Jesus was, "Kill them all." Satan's knowledge is limited. When God hides someone, Satan can't find them. It has been Satan's strategy to kill all by mass murder, genocide. Hitler, Pol Pot, Mussolini, Stalin—all evil men controlled by Satan. Why? Satan knows that there are many men and women of God that are a threat to his evil plan to control the whole world. So naturally, abortion fits in perfectly with Satan's plan. How many? Sixty three million abortions! How many potential pastors, prophets, missionaries, evangelists? How many scientists, doctors, lawyers, teachers, nurses, and counselors?

Their blood cries out from the hospital garbage cans, the abortion mills that make people rich. The broken limbs and bodies, perfectly formed in the womb, tossed out with the rest of the trash. They are so consumed with greed that they sell the body parts.

> "Rejoice over her, thou heaven, and ye holy apostles and prophets; for God hath avenged you on her" (Rev. 18:20).
> "And cried when they saw the smoke of her burning, saying, 'What city is like unto this great city?'" (Rev. 18:18).

I pray that Christians wake up before it's too late, but I fear it is already too late. God hears the cry of the slaughter of the innocents. He will do something soon to stop the genocide of a whole generation.

> "Babylon the great is fallen, is fallen, and is become the habitation of devils" (Rev. 18:2).

Stand up and voice your concern. If you are pro-choice, then repent for you are progenocide, pro-murder.

Repent, repent, repent, repent! In the Name of Jesus Christ, repent! Amen.

What Is Wrong with Christians?

> "The thief cometh not, but for to steal, and to kill, and to destroy: I am come that they might have life, and that they might have it more abundantly" (John 10:10).
>
> "And if a kingdom be divided against itself, that kingdom cannot stand" (Mark 3:24).
>
> "But he that shall blaspheme against the Holy Ghost hath never forgiveness, but is in danger of eternal damnation: Because they said, he hath an unclean spirit" (Mark 3:29, 30).

Satan has entered the minds of some Christian leaders to cause division. This is why there are so many different Christian religions. Although there are many different Christian religions, there is only one true body of Christ. This is possible because God knows the person by their heart and by their prayers and their inner personal relationship with him, Jesus Christ.

Division of Christians is from the devil. Jesus would have us all united. The most powerful bond of unity is love for all. That is why Jesus taught us to love one another, love thy neighbor, and even to love thine enemies. If it was Jesus that delivered you from darkness, then glorify His name with your testimony. Show the world the fruits of the Spirit and cherish the gifts also.

If you don't believe in the gifts or think that healing is not for today, then at least acknowledge the fruits of the Spirit and let those be manifested in your life. Not everyone has enough faith to believe all things from Christ, but we should not let that divide us. If the Catholics, Protestants, born-again believers, Missionary Alliance, Church of God, Assemblies of God, Independents, Baptists,

Messianic Jews, and any other religion that believes that Jesus Christ is the only begotten Son of God by whom all must receive to be saved could all unite and come together for one cause, we would be unstoppable and would push back against the gates of hell.

I call on everyone to elevate the Name of Jesus Christ. Someday every knee will bow to give glory to His Name. One day there will be nothing to divide the people of God. Someday Jesus will return to reign as king over all the earth. Amen.

What Is Wrong with Catholics?

> "And call no man your father upon the earth: for one is your father, which is in heaven" (Matt. 23:9)

The Catholics call the priests Father and the pope is called the Holy Father.

> "Thou shalt not make thee any graven image, or any likeness of anything that is in heaven above, or that is in the earth beneath, or that is in the waters beneath the earth" (Deut. 5:8).

The Catholic churches are full of graven images and are worshipped as if they were something alive and holy. Some Catholics pray to these statues, hoping to see tears come out of their wooden eyes. What an evil expectation. Where does their hope lie, in wood and plaster?

> "Thou shalt not bow down thyself unto them, nor serve them: for I the Lord thy God am a jealous God, visiting the iniquity of the fathers upon the children unto the third and fourth generation of them that hate me" (Deut. 5:9).

When Christ was crucified, the veil in the temple was torn open, signifying that access to God was available through His Son,

Jesus Christ. We need no other mediator to go to God. We don't need a priest or rabbi or nun or pastor. When you get on your knees and pray to God the Father in the name of Jesus Christ, you have a direct connection.

> "And he took bread and gave thanks, and brake it, and gave unto them saying, This is My body which is given for you: this do in remembrance of Me" (Luke 22:19).

All Christians, after examining themselves and if they feel worthy, should take communion out of respect for Christ and also do it in remembrance of Christ. Now you can use bread, crackers, croutons, wine, grape juice, apple juice, it really doesn't matter because these are mere symbols of remembrance and nothing more. The Catholic priests teach that the host or Eucharist is the actual and literal body of Christ. Let's look at reality, not fables.

> "For we have not followed cunningly devised fables, when we made known unto you the power and coming of our Lord Jesus Christ, but were eyewitnesses of his majesty" (2 Pet. 1:16).

Lord Jesus, show us your truth in all that you taught your disciples when you walked the streets of Jerusalem two thousand years ago. Amen.

The Virgin Mary

> "And Mary said, Behold the handmaid of the Lord: be it unto me according to thy word. And the angel departed from her" (Luke 1:38).

God found favor with Mary, and she was a virgin. The Holy Ghost came upon her, and the power of the Highest did overshadow her, and Mary became pregnant with the baby Jesus. Mary and Joseph married and had several other children after Jesus was born.

Mary was blessed by God and deserves our utmost respect, but Mary was only human. As such, she had no special powers. It is wrong to pray to Mary or any other human being, living or dead. It is idolatry to make statues of Mary and kneel before it to pay homage. It is wrong to pray the rosary or pray to Catholic saints or burn candles or incense to any of these statues.

It is Jesus Christ that deserves our complete worship. His mother was a blessed vessel of the Most High God; but as another human being, Mary needed to acknowledge Jesus, not as her son but as her Lord and Savior. She too needed to repent and be baptized in the name of the Father, Son, and Hoy Ghost. The Bible tells us that all have sinned.

"For all have sinned, and come short of the glory of God" (Rom. 3:23).

The early Catholic Church, the Church of Rome, forced other Christians to swear an oath to worship Mary and those that refused were tortured and put to death. Their names are recorded in a book entitled *Foxe's Book of Martyrs*. I am sure the Vatican has many records archived that describe such atrocities committed by the Church of Rome against the true Christians.

I pray for all Catholics to read the Bible and let the truth set you free! Amen.

Six, Six, Six (666)

"And he had power to give life unto the image of the beast, that the image of the beast should both speak and cause that as many as would not worship the image of the beast should be killed" (Rev. 13:15).

"Nebuchadnezzar the king made an image of gold whose height was threescore cubits and the breadth thereof six cubits: he set it up in the plain of Dura, in the province of Babylon. And whoso falleth not down and worshippeth shall the same hour be cast into the midst of a burning fiery furnace" (Dan. 3:1, 6).

History has a habit of repeating itself. When the people turn from God and give their power to a king or a government, then eventually the devil steps in and takes control. What the people see as freedom will eventually become slavery. What happens when the government becomes too big and too powerful is imposition of laws that restrict freedom of speech, laws and taxes upon taxes, to feed the beast that comes to life. When the beast comes to life, it becomes mad with power and eventually causes all to worship and accept its laws. Help us, Lord Jesus! Amen.

Trust in Christ 100 Percent

"Whosoever shall seek to save his life shall lose it; and whosoever shall lose his life shall preserve it. Two men shall be in the field; the one shall be taken, and the other left" (Luke 17:33, 36).

Most Christians know that we are living in the end time that Jesus talked about in the Gospels. Many people look for new signs that will appear. Some say we should stock up on food, water, and other survival-type goods. To have a little extra put up for emergencies is a wise thing to do, but do not go to extremes. The reason why you should not have too much stored up is because when Jesus returns for His Bride, the Church (the body of believers), it will happen very quickly. You will have to make a choice quickly also.

Do I run inside and hunker down with my MREs and my guns, or do I look up to the sky and raise my hands and say, "Take me home, Lord Jesus"?

Some people prepare to save their body but fail to prepare their soul.

The rich spend lots of money to save themselves. They build bomb shelter and stock up food, water, weapons, ammunition, gold, and silver. Why? Because they want to survive to live another day, to sin another day. People that focus on surviving the day of Christ's return will need all those things they stockpiled in their basements. They will be glad they did when they realize they were left behind. Now they will have to go through seven years of hell on earth. They will have to live during the Tribulation. They put their trust in material things instead of God.

The book of Revelation describes God's judgment being poured out on the earth. A time for people to repent. A time of a one-world government that will hunt down and kill anyone that refuses to receive the mark of the beast, 666.

The Lord has shown me not to stockpile food but pray and fast and stockpile the Word of God in my mind. To be ready to leave this world in a minute's notice.

Remember Lot's wife (Luke 17:32).

Come quickly, Lord Jesus, I am ready to leave this world, and go to a much better place. Amen.

The Narrow Path

> "There is therefore now no condemnation to them which are in Christ Jesus, who walk not after the flesh, but after the Spirit" (Rom. 8:1).

Once you have decided you want to follow Christ and walk the narrow path, you will notice a series of changes in your life. As you are led by the Holy Spirit, you will experience more peace and joy. You will also feel conviction by the Spirit when you feel temptation to sin or when you fall into sin; and you will from time to time as we are only human and not perfect. Each time we fall into sin, it is another time of testing our resolve to be more like Christ and less like the world. Don't give up; never quit trying. The battle is not over until we die and meet the Lord.

Because of this process of cleansing the soul by submission to the Holy Spirit, there is no condemnation, only conviction. For God is a merciful and understanding God. He knows it is difficult to transition from flesh to spirit in a world full of evil temptation.

However, I have a problem with Christians that quote only half of Bible verses. Some quote only the first part and say, "There is therefore now no condemnation to them which are in Christ Jesus." They left out the part, "Who walk not after the flesh, but after the Spirit." You cannot take any scripture and use it to justify sin. Sin is the flesh, the world, and the devil. Let's make no mistake about that. We are in a battle for our lives, our souls.

> "For everyone shall be salted with fire, and every
> sacrifice shall be salted with salt" (Mark 9:49).

If you desire to walk the narrow path with Christ, you have chosen a good thing. I pray for strength to overcome all evil in life's journey. Amen.

An Example

> "Let no man despise thy youth; but be thou an
> example of the believers, in word, in conversa-
> tion, in charity, in spirit, in faith, in purity. Till I
> come, give attendance to reading, to exhortation,
> to doctrine" (1 Tim. 4:12, 13).

No one wants to be judged by others or talked about or ridiculed, especially by those that are lost. No one said it would be easy to walk with Christ. Let me rephrase that and say, it is easy if we walk with Christ. What is hard is controlling old habits and being a good example as a Christian. We are in a battle, flesh against spirit. We must strive to watch what we say in conversation. God, we pray to purify our conversation as an example to others and for ourselves. Amen.

> "Iron sharpeneth iron, so a man sharpeneth the countenance of his friend" (Prov. 27:17).

It can be hard to find fellowship with other Christians in a small-group setting, but not impossible. Keep looking. Be careful though, there are wolves in sheep's clothing that will present themselves as Christians just to gain your confidence. Then they will lead you down a path of slavery to their hidden agenda. The sad thing is that most of these people are sincere, thinking they are doing the will of God. The truth is they have been brainwashed and are victims of their own devices.

The important thing to remember is that Jesus said, "I am the truth, and the truth will set you free." Not free to live in sin, but free from living in sin. No one is perfect, and they know this. Some will use this to put you under guilt and condemnation in order to make you feel like you need to be subservient to their hidden agenda, which almost always involves giving them your time, your money, and your free labor. In other words, slavery that is legal because it is voluntary. The most effective form of brainwashing someone is to allow them the freedom to convince themselves. It is the subliminal suggestions that will patiently break down a person's will.

The sad thing is that they prey on the people that have a desire to do whatever is required of them to please God but are misdirected and uninformed as to what Jesus taught. That is why the Bible is needed as our source of enlightenment and power. There is power in the Word of God.

Beware of religions that are always trying to push other books for you to read instead of the Bible.

The purpose of my book, *The Narrow Path*, is to encourage you to read your Bible, and pray, and talk to God. And I am confident that your life will be better. Amen.

Sin Willfully?

> "For if we sin willfully after that we have received the knowledge of the truth, there remaineth no more sacrifice for sins, But a certain fearful look-

ing for of judgment and fiery indignation, which
shall devour the adversaries" (Heb. 10:26).

Jesus suffered and died a horrible, painful death on the cross
for our sins so that when we receive Jesus into ourselves, we become
cleansed of all unrighteousness. This is such a free gift by the grace of
God that to fully appreciate it is impossible, but to contemplate its
meaning and to meditate on this is enough to know that it was the
complete and only sacrifice that the world will ever have in all eternity. There is no other sacrifice needed or acceptable to God.

When we fall into temptation of the devil, we need to fall on
our knees and repent. The more we repent, the stronger we become
until we are free from those sins.

But to willfully sin, after receiving the knowledge of the truth
set forth by the Bible, is a very bad place to be. It is equal to spitting
on Christ as he carried His cross up the hill to Calvary. Lord, help
us! Amen.

Love and Hate

"Hate the evil and love the good, and establish
judgment in the gate: it may be that the Lord
of hosts will be gracious unto the remnant of
Joseph" (Amos 5:15).

According to the Bible, its teachings require us to hate evil and
love the good. We are in a battle for our lives, a battle that will determine what kind of civilization our future generations will inherit.

Sometimes I am weary of hearing we are living in the last days,
even though I find myself saying this! My point being this, if we
knew for a certainty that Christ would return in ten years, how different would or should our mission be than if we knew for certain
that our Lord will return in five hundred years from now?

If the Lord's return be ten years, then hold on tight and brace
yourself. But if the Lord's return be five hundred years, then ask yourself, how can I be effective to help rid the world of evil for the future

generations? We are all here for a purpose. Can you go to your grave knowing that your life has made this world a better place for someone else now and five hundred years from now? I pray it will! Amen.

The Dumb Ass Speaks

Read Numbers 22:20–27.

> "And the Lord opened the mouth of the ass, and she said unto Balaam, What have I done unto thee, that thou hast smitten me these three times?" (Num. 22:28).

The Lord has a path. It is narrow, and few can find it. Once on this path, the devil will entice you to step off the path and take another way. Now the Lord will do many things to warn us when we stray off His path. In the Bible verse above, Balaam is an example of one of God's servants that could not discern the will of God. Balaam didn't want to go where God wanted him to go. Balaam was following his flesh instead of the spirit. That is why he couldn't see the angel of the Lord blocking his path. Balaam was so frustrated with his donkey that he beat her three times with his staff. Sometimes we can get so frustrated that we feel like beating someone. That is when we need to open our spiritual eyes so we can stay on the path the God has directed us to walk down.

The angel of the Lord went out to change the intention of the heart of Balaam. The Lord wanted to help Balaam so much that he showed the angel to the donkey and in so doing frightened the donkey enough to change directions and eventually stop and fall down under Balaam. When the donkey spoke to Balaam, Balaam's eyes were finally opened to see the angel of the Lord standing in the way with his sword drawn in his hand. Balaam didn't know how close he came to being killed. It took an animal talking to get his attention.

Isn't God merciful to His servants? How many times has God warned us, his servants, to not follow after evil but to turn away from evil and stay on the narrow path? What would you do if your pets started talking? Sometimes God will do great things to keep His people safe.

I pray that Jesus guides us daily. Amen.

Commit Thy Way

> "Delight thyself also in the Lord; and He shall give thee the desires of thine heart. Commit thy way unto the Lord; trust also in him and He shall bring it to pass" (Ps. 37:4, 5).

Commit means to pledge, to bind, to commit oneself to a certain coarse (Webster's Dictionary).

One thing I have learned is that when a Bible verse stands out and speaks to your spirit, it is good to read the next verse too. So many times people pick and choose what Bible verses they like and apply just those that in reality are only half-truths. That is what Satan did when he tempted Jesus in the desert. That is why we need to get the whole truth of scripture, not just half truths.

I have heard Christians say, God will give you the desires of your heart or name it and claim it, but as we read Psalm 37:5, we learn that first we must commit our life to the Lord. Now that is not a small matter. I could write a book on that verse alone.

God is a God of order. Satan is the author of confusion. We must do things in an orderly and planned-out way. You have to have a plan, and in that plan you have to set before you a list of priorities. You also have to have the knowledge of God's moral requirements.

For instance, if the desire of your heart is to fill your needs, due to being lonely, your flesh may desire to have an affair. Let's go to God's word and see if this is permissible. The Bible says adultery and fornication are deadly sins, so the answer from God is, "No, I will not give you that desire of your heart." But if your way is committed to the Lord and your desire is to fill the void of loneliness, then God will give you a mate. You must be willing to wait for a Christian that will be compatible so that you will not be unequally yoked, as the Bible warns believers.

So if you do everything according to the Bible and commit yourself to the Lord, you can ask for the desires of your heart with confidence. If it is good for you, God will assist you in achieving your goals. If everything seems to go wrong, then it probably was something that God knew would not be good for you. Whatever your heart's desire is, you must use wisdom and pray because you have an adversary, the devil, that wants you to be miserable and feel defeated. So always pray for God's will to be done. That way nothing is impossible. Also be careful for what you pray for because you just might get it. And along with answered prayers comes godly responsibilities that you may not have been aware of at the time of your request. Amen.

When Mary Met Jesus

> "Now when Jesus was risen early the first day of the week, he appeared first to Mary Magdalene, out of whom He had cast seven devils" (Mark 16:9).
>
> "And certain women, which had been healed of evil spirits and infirmities, Mary called Magdalene, out of whom went seven devils" (Luke 8:2).

Jesus cast out seven devils from Mary Magdalene. The Bible does not tell us anymore about that, but Mary Magdalene was a follower of Jesus and she was the first person that saw the risen Christ. She also loved Jesus very much, so it is safe to say that Mary was as devoted to Jesus as were the apostles.

Now as for the seven devils, we don't know what they were about. Some speculate that Mary was a prostitute, but another possibility is Mary may have had physical and mental disabilities. Many times when Jesus cast out a devil from someone, they were either deaf, dumb, or blind. After Jesus cast out the devil, they were healed of their disability. The seven devils could be a combination of disabilities and sinful behavior.

Mary met Jesus as he went throughout every city and village preaching the good news of the kingdom of God and casting out devils and healing the sick. In an instant, a miracle happened to Mary. She was completely healed and set free! She was made whole!

No wonder Mary loved Jesus so much. She followed Him and was devoted to His teachings. Can Jesus heal people today like he did two thousand years ago? I believe all things are possible to those that have faith. Mary had the faith. Jesus had the power; and when they met face-to-face, she was totally and instantly healed, set free, delivered, and made whole. She was a new Christian, born again, transformed forever. Jesus doesn't do temporary, partial healings. When you meet Jesus face-to-face, you walk away a different person! Amen.

Kingdom Power

"For the Kingdom of God is not in word, but in power" (1 Cor. 4:20).

The Bible is much more than words written on paper, the Word of God is power to them that believe. By faith we believe the Word. The more faith we have in the Word of God, the more we read and learn. Faith is believing in what we do not see or feel. An example would be believing God for your physical healing when you see no improvement. Now that takes faith.

The above Bible verse refers to the church at Corinth. Paul says they have speech that is puffed up. That is why he says the Kingdom of God is not about prideful, puffed-up words and speeches. Paul reminds them of the power of God that is manifested in the true church. Is there power in your church? Do they teach and read from the Bible?

People have testimonies as to how they have been healed and delivered from addictions, set free from all sorts of ailments, depression, and grief. Now that is the power of God that is alive in some Christian churches. That is where Jesus is exalted and the Bible is preached.

Thank you, Lord Jesus, for the power of your Word. Amen.

Judge Yourself

"For he that eateth and drinketh unworthily, eateth and drinketh damnation to himself, not discerning the Lord's body. For this cause many are weak and sickly among you, and many sleep. For if we judge yourselves, we should not be judged. But when we are judged, we are chastened of the Lord, that we should not be condemned with the world" (1 Cor. 11:29–32)

As we study God's Word, we learn what is sinful and displeasing to God. If we are active in serious sin, we should refrain from receiving the body and blood of Christ, out of reverence and fear for the holiness of our Lord. Communion is a serious part of Christianity. Examine yourself, judge yourself, show yourself worthy to partake. For God will not be mocked. There is no scripture found that allows sin in the church. Sin is an evil that needs to be purged from the Christian, and the Bible teaches to judge yourself and repent. Those that refuse to repent are judged of the Lord and punished in the body, even unto death. Those that escape this chastisement of the Lord and continue in sin and even teach others to sin receive eternal damnation.

Lord, save us! Lord, protect us! Lord, heal us! Amen.

Judgment Day

"For the Father judgeth no man, but hath committed all judgment unto the Son" (John 5:22).

"And Jesus said, For judgment I am come into this world, that they which see not might see; and they which see might be made blind" (John 9:39).

"For God sent not his Son into the world to condemn the world; but that the world through Him might be saved" (John 3:17).

Jesus came two thousand years ago to offer forgiveness of sins. He preached repentance and baptism. He preached to heal and set the captive free. He gave grace to man. The world has been under God's grace for over two thousand years. Like the grace period when you have an extra ten days to pay a bill after the due date, our whole life is a grace period with God. I believe as long as a person is alive, there is hope for them to accept the Lord. When Jesus came, He came as a way for us to avoid the judgment for our sins that we repent of, not so we can continue to live in sin.

Jesus is coming back to bring judgment to the world. He will be an advocate for His sheep. Are you a sheep of Jesus's flock?

As our advocate, Jesus will say all your sins that you have repented of are erased from my memory. Isn't that wonderful? That is like a criminal with a long arrest record going before the judge and the judge saying this man is truly repentant, therefore, destroy his past arrest record and let's give him a fresh start and a new life. A blank record. But if after that the criminal goes out and murders and robs the innocent and he goes before that same judge, that judge will be angry and will pronounce a harsh sentence.

Jesus is coming back, soon I hope. When Jesus comes back at the last trumpet blast, at that moment the grace period will end. Just like the moment the door to Noah's Ark was closed by the hand of God.

> "And as it was in the days of No'e, so shall it be also in the days of the Son of man. They did eat, they drank, they married wives, they were given in marriage, until the day that No'e entered into the ark, and the flood came, and destroyed them all"(Luke 17:26, 27).
>
> "For yourselves know perfectly that the day of the Lord so cometh as a thief in the night" (1 Thess. 5:2).

Are you ready to face judgment? Pray every day, as if there will be no tomorrow. Amen.

Blessings and Curses

"The memory of the just is blessed: but the name of the wicked shall rot" (Prov. 10:7).

"And afterward he read all the words of the law, the blessings and cursings, according to all that was written in the book of the law" (Josh. 8:34).

If you are doing everything in line with the Bible and use wisdom in your finances and give your offerings, then don't worry when hard times come because God is on your side. God will take care of you and your family. Those under your covering your anointing, that is. You may have family members grown up, living on their own, they have to go to God for their own blessings.

Our God is a personal God. He knows the number of hairs on your head. There can also be a blessing on a town or nation, depending on how many people come together in unity for God's blessings. The bad news is that a city or a nation can fall under the curses as a result of rebellion against God. If the rebellion grows faster than revival, then evil will take hold and change laws to allow more evil to spread.

The Christian can still be under God's protection and blessings, although at some point the balance of power may shift to an evil majority. When that happens to a nation, then God may lift His anointing and protection and that can put God's people in danger. You may think that doesn't seem fair, but it is a direct result of a shift toward evil due to lack of commitment on behalf of the Christian community, or lack of leadership, or lack of holiness, or all three.

The best way to build up the Body of Christ is a personal spiritual revival, self-assessment as to priorities, and renewal of personal holiness with Jesus Christ. Take the time to read the Bible and apply it to your life—one day at a time, one life at a time. Like drops of rain coming together to form a mighty ocean.

If revival doesn't come, someday you will find yourself kneeling before an idol.

Help us, Lord. Purify our hearts. Amen.

The Lord Is My Strength

> "Behold, God is my salvation, I will trust and not be afraid: for the Lord, JEHOVAH, is my strength and my song; he also is become my salvation" (Isa. 12:2).
>
> "The way of the Lord is strength to the upright: but destruction shall be to the workers of iniquity" (Prov. 10:29).

No matter what state of health you find yourself in, you can be strengthened by God's Word. Even if you have prayed daily and see no results in your condition improving, hang on tight to the spiritual things of God. For God is spirit, and so are we, once we are born again by His spirit.

It is God's desire that no one perish, but Jesus doesn't force us to believe. Everyone must die a physical death, with the exception of those who are alive at the time of the Rapture. They will not die a physical death. Our spirits will live on for eternity where there will be no pain or sorrow, where Jesus will wipe away every tear from our eyes. Heaven will be beautiful, beyond anything we could ever imagine.

If you live to be one hundred years old, your whole life would be just one raindrop in the ocean compared to eternity with God. So think in terms of life everlasting, and walk in a manner worthy of a Christian.

Pray for the strength to say no to the devil and yes to the things of God. How much time and money have you invested in television, movies, computers, and phones? All these devices will be burned up in the Day of the Lord. The only things that will remain are the things of God and the things that we have done for people, for God, and for ourselves that edify Jesus Christ, our Lord.

There will be rewards for the faithful and punishment for evil. For people that consider themselves good people, without God in their lives, there will be a day that burns like an oven. A blast of fire will proceed from the throne of God and burn up everything that is material or neutral. That person will stand before a Holy God with nothing, not even any clothes. No money, no car, no boat, no houses, no gold, no silver, no stocks, no bonds, no relatives, no nothing; and God will say to His Son, Jesus, "Do you know this one?" And Jesus will say, "No! I never knew him (or her)." And God will cast that person down into hell for all eternity.

> "Behold, I stand at the door and knock: if any man hear My voice and open the door, I will come in to him and will sup with him and he with Me" (Rev. 3:20).

Lord Jesus, strengthen us, for we are one body! Amen.

Share a Little

> "And Elijah said unto her, Fear not; go and do as thou hast said: but make me thereof a little cake first, and bring it unto me, and after make for thee and thy son" (1 Kings 17:13).
> "But he said unto them, Give ye them to eat. And they said, we have no more but five loaves and two fishes; except we should go and buy meat for all this people" (Luke 9:13).

The time to share is now, not someday after you become rich. The reason is due to the many examples in the Bible of people sharing the little bit they had to help others and to sow into the Kingdom of God the seeds of faith so that God could multiply it many times.

They gave out of love, compassion, and obedience, not so they could receive a reward. We must examine our motives and be honest with ourselves. Some false preachers teach people to give so they can get back ten or one hundredfold. So they give to that preacher, and he gets rich, and they get poor and mad at God. What a farce!

Jesus said, if you see your brother without a coat and you have two coats, give one to him. This is brotherly love. Don't be a hoarder.

Ask yourself this: Do I have enough? How much do I really need? When greed takes control of your life, you can never have enough. In that mind-set you will not be happy because you will not be content with what you have. Always wanting bigger, better, more and more.

When you die you go to the grave with one suit of clothing. How many people in the world go to bed hungry? How would you feel if when you turned on the television and saw the faces of the starving children in other countries crying out for food, and all of a sudden you saw your mother or father or sister or brother mixed in with the crowd, begging for food?

Jesus said whenever you give to the poor, you are giving to Him. Whenever you withhold from the poor, you withhold from Him.

Giving and sharing is love in action. It is a mind-set that is present in the poorest of the poor or the richest of the rich. Selfishness can also be a mind-set. Rich and poor is defined by the context of their society. A person on welfare in the United States of America is rich compared to the poor of India or Africa. Some millionaires consider themselves poor when comparing themselves to billionaires. And the Holy Grail of achievement for a billionaire would to be a trillionaire.

Which one are you? The sharer, the hoarder, or the thief? What we do in our life will follow us to the Judgment!

Help us, Lord Jesus. Amen.

True Martyrs for God

> "And when He had opened the fifth seal, I saw under the alter the souls of them that were slain for the Word of God, and for the testimony which they held" (Rev. 6:9).

The true Christians were killed in horrible ways, and since the days of the apostles until now, Christians around the world are being persecuted and killed. These are true martyrs for God. In order to be a martyr, you first must be a Christian. All others are imposters. You also must be put to death by unbelievers or Christian imposters for the Word of God, which is Jesus Christ and the Bible and for your testimony. Your testimony is your personal story as to how you received Christ and were born again.

In *Foxes Book of Martyrs* are stories of those Christians who have been put to death for their faith in Christ. You don't have to be educated or have accomplished great things in life to be a martyr. All you have to do is to be a born-again Christian and to stand up for what you believe. If you do that, the evil people in the world will hate you. They will rise up and persecute you and even put you to death. Why? Because Satan hates God, and if you receive Jesus, you are a child of God. Satan who lives in the world and controls anyone that is not a Christian will instruct anyone to kill Christians. Satan will also kill anyone and everyone because he is a murderer. Anyone that hates Christians can read what Jesus has to say about them in John 8:44.

> "Ye are of your father the devil, and the lusts of your father ye will do. He was a murderer from the beginning, and abode not in the truth, because there is no truth in him. When he speaketh a lie, he speaketh of his own: for he is a liar, and the father of it" (John 8:44).
>
> "And I saw the souls of them that were beheaded for the witness of Jesus, and for the Word of God" (Rev. 20:4).

Now there will come a time of great tribulation and persecution of Christians by a world leader whose number is 666. Those that refuse to worship the beast will be beheaded.

There is a major religion in the world that claims to be peaceful, but they go around judging people and their favorite form of punishment is beheading. They claim to be martyrs when they kill themselves in a suicide mission, thinking falsely that they will be rewarded with all these virgins in heaven. What they don't realize is, the Christians that they kill will be the real martyrs that will be rewarded in heaven. Those led by Satan will return to Satan in hell where they will burn for eternity and where the worms never die.

If you are one of these, then your only hope is to repent and ask Jesus to be your Lord and Savior. I pray that God will open your eyes to the truth. God is a God of love, and to be a true follower of God is to voluntarily walk the narrow path of Christ. All other paths lead to hell.

I pray for the Lord Jesus to reveal himself to the lost in a dream or vision. Amen.

The Mission

> "The Lord said unto my Lord, sit thou at my right hand, until I make thine enemies thy footstool" (Ps. 110:1).
> "The Lord hath sworn, and will not repent, Thou art a priest forever after the order of Melchizedek" (Ps. 110:4).

The Lord of Heaven and Earth is Jesus Christ. Those that make Jesus their Lord over their lives have become a royal priest like unto the order of Melchizedek. As a born-again Christian, we are grafted into the Vine. We are children of God. As God's children, we are privileged and we have an inheritance to look forward to. We are a part of a Kingdom that will be ruling the earth with Jesus as King over all the earth. All the kingdoms of the earth will be under the Lordship of Jesus.

This is not pie in the sky by and by. This is a war that has been raging for thousands of years, good against evil. It is every Christian's duty to fight against evil in this life as a preparation for things to come. We all need to pray for the elimination of evils such as alcohol, drugs, tobacco, pornography, inequality, false religions. Jesus Christ is the One and Only Truth! Amen.

Tell the Truth

> "Ye are of your father the devil, and the lusts of your father you will do. He was a murderer from the beginning, and abode not in the truth,

because there is no truth in him. When he speaketh a lie, he speaketh of his own: for he is a liar,
and the father of it" (John 8:44).

The devil is the father of lies. If you are a liar, then you are full
of the devil. Turn or burn, the choice is yours. You cannot serve two
masters. Jesus said, "You will love one and hate the other."

"For without are dogs, and sorcerers, and whore-
mongers, and murderers and idolaters, and whosoever loveth and maketh a lie" (Rev. 22:15).

Some people love to make up lies. This can be so destructive
and cause much damage to lives. A lie can destroy a person's reputa-
tion. A lie can spread a rumor that can destroy a church or ministry.
This is why God takes this sin so seriously. Repent while you can.
Then make amends to those you have hurt with your lies. When
Jesus returns, it will be too late to repent.
Lord, help us tame our tongues. Amen.

Order in the Court!

"And he was clothed with a vesture dipped in
blood: and His name is called the Word of God.
And he hath on his vesture and on his thigh a
name written, *King of kings, and Lord of lords*"
(Rev. 19:13, 16).
"And he shall rule them with a rod of iron"
(Rev. 19:15).

Jesus will return with power to judge and rule the entire earth.
He will wipe away every tear from our eyes. He will judge our every
thought, and he will rule with a rod of iron.
Can you imagine yourself standing before Jesus, He knowing
your every thought and looking into your very soul with eyes like

fire. You can't run or hide or lie. You will be transparent and unable to stand in His presence.

For every knee will bow and every tongue will confess that Jesus Christ is Lord. *Every* means all! For you Muslims, Hindus, Jehovah Witnesses, Mormons, all you atheists, humanists, Satanists, witches, yes, *all*, including myself, will fall at His feet and tremble. His glory will be awesome on that wonderful Day that He returns to rule the world. Amen.

Friend or Servant?

> "Henceforth I call you not servants; for the servant knoweth not what his lord doeth: but I have called you friends; for all things that I have heard of my father I have made known unto you" (John 15:15).
>
> "If ye keep My commandments, ye shall abide in my love" (John 15:10).

The good news that Jesus gives his disciples is that after a time of spiritual cleansing and obedience to His commandments, their relationship with Jesus changes from one of servant to that of friend.

We are not to deceive ourselves. If you do not keep His commandments, you are not His friend and you will not abide in His love. This is that narrow path that Jesus talked about. We must strive to purge all evil from our lives, not just those things that are easy or easily covered up.

The reason for personal purity is the difference between being a servant or a friend of Jesus. The servant has the attitude of doing this or that and leaving. The friend has the attitude of doing this or that and staying to enjoy the fellowship of closeness. This is the personal love we have for Jesus, and it leads to a deeper spiritual meaning.

There are different levels of personal relationships. Some have more depth and meaning than others. For example, Joe meets the mayor of the city at a dinner party and shakes his hand and says hello. The next day Joe says to his friend at work, "I know the mayor, yeah. We are good friends" or "I know the mayor, and he is a close friend of mine." The truth is the mayor meets so many people that he doesn't even remember Joe's name.

Joe was also in the army. He had a friend in basic training. They both went to Vietnam and spent a lot of time together. They talked about many personal subjects and helped each other on assignments. One day Joe took a bullet for his friend. That is the ultimate expression of brotherly love. This is what Jesus refers to in the following verse:

> "Greater love hath no man than this, that a man
> lay down his life for his friends" (John 15:13).

If you want to be a friend to Jesus, you have to take a bullet for him and kill your fleshly desires. That means you must die to yourself and think of what is best for someone other than yourself.

Help us, cleanse us, and purify us, Lord Jesus. Amen.

Beware of Cults

> "For many shall come in my name, saying, I am
> Christ; and shall deceive you" (Matt. 24:5).
> "And many false prophets shall rise, and
> shall deceive many" (Matt. 24:11).

If you go to a Christian bookstore, you can find a section on cults. You will be surprised to see a lot of popular denominations referred to as cults.

My opinion as to what defines a cult is any group, religion, secret society, club, organization, or even political movement that has an agenda of controlling its members. I will not go into the subject of mind control at this time due to the complexities of that subject, but controlling is definitely a sign of a cult. Remember that Jesus came to set the captive free.

Another sign of a cult is they will claim to have discovered or been enlightened with a secret knowledge that was lost over the centuries or a secret that has been handed down by divine revelation. As a result, they have other books for you to study other than the Bible. These books will lead you down a path that will take you away from Jesus Christ. What can be confusing is that a lot of these cults use the name of Jesus Christ, but they worship devils that appeared to be angels.

A third sign to look for is the appeal to pride. They will make you feel that you have been given special knowledge and wisdom that will separate you from the rest of humanity that is lost. They will show you some secret that was revealed to their leader or founder something that no one else could see or figure out. And this something could even be taken out of the Christian Bible and taken out of context yet used to build a whole new religion. You can't build a religion based on one or two verses from the bible.

I believe that the King James Bible translated in 1611 is the most accurate version of the Word of God. I believe the Bible has the power of the Holy Spirit. Yes, there are some parts that seem hard to understand, but you can find some good study guides to help you or get in a good Bible study group at your church. But the Word that Jesus gives to us does not take a PhD to understand it. The whole purpose of the Bible is to draw us closer to God the Father and the Lord, Jesus Christ, to turn away from sin and live a life worthy of our calling.

Picture in your mind just two people in the whole world—you and Jesus Christ. That is what is needed in the world, a personal relationship with our Lord and Savior. You will know when you are serving the true Christ because His holiness will convict you of all sin in your life from which He wants you to repent. All these other books and cults are debris that will come between you and Christ.

Don't run "from Jesus," run "to Jesus" no matter what. Amen.

Prepare Thyself

"And ye shall seek me, and find me, when ye shall search for me with all your heart" (Jer. 29:13).

It should be everyone's lifelong quest to seek and find Jesus Christ and, once He is found, to walk the narrow path all the days of our life. Below is a checklist to see if you are on that narrow path:

1. Accept Jesus as Savior (Born Again)
2. Baptized by immersion
3. Member of Bible preaching/teaching church
4. Active in the church
5. Be a cheerful and generous giver to your church
6. Support missions
7. Be charitable to the less fortunate
8. Love thy neighbor
9. Love thy enemies
10. Read and study the Bible daily
11. Pray daily
12. Not ashamed of Christ, openly confess Christ to others
13. Take a personal, moral inventory often
14. Turn away from sin
15. Take a stand against sin wherever it is found
16. Get involved with your government to elect godly leaders
17. Glorify Jesus Christ as God come in the flesh

Everyone has a secret sin in their life, the one or two things that no one knows about. God wants you to give it up. He has a special blessing for you if you give it up to Him as a sacrifice.

Lord Jesus, deliver us from all sin in our life. Keep us on the narrow path that is life everlasting. Help us to change our nation and our world for the peace and safety of future generations. Lord Jesus, purge us from all evil—evil in us, our nation, and our world. We thank you, Lord, for saving us by your blood on the cross. Amen.

Why, Dear God, Why?

August 6, 2018
Yesterday was a hot day, and my wife and I and our friend's daughter Sara, went for a walk along the Erie Canal. This was after

church, but it was so hot and humid that we decided to go home and have ice cream. So we each picked our favorite ice cream from the freezer and sat on the couch to finish watching the movie that we started previously. *I Can Only Imagine* was the name of the movie. It was an emotional story, and my mind was being flooded with memories of the past that made me think of my nephew Christopher, who had visited us just two weeks ago. I thought this would be a good movie for him to watch, hoping it would help him in his struggle with addictions.

As I was thinking on this and half of my attention was on the movie (This was my third time watching it), all of a sudden my phone rang. It was my sister, Marcia. As soon as I heard her sobbing request for prayer, I remembered the other phone calls of the past. The phone calls that no parent ever wants to hear. It was all too familiar. Another death in the family.

"Marcia, what's wrong?" I asked.

"Oh, Eli, I am on my way to Christopher's. Tell everyone to pray for Christopher. They are saying he is dead, but I believe Jesus can raise him up!"

Christopher, 35

Richard, 33

John, 35

Lynn, 35

Kim, 37

Jennifer, 35

David, 53

"Jesus saith unto her, "I am the resurrection, and the life: he that believeth in me, though he were dead, yet shall he live: And whosoever liveth and believeth in me shall never die. Believest thou this?" (John 11:25, 26).

"Blessed are they that mourn: for they shall be comforted" (Matt. 5:4).

The Passive Power of Christ

> "And Herod with his men of war set him at naught, and mocked him, and arrayed him in a gorgeous robe, and sent him again to Pilate. And the same day, Pilate and Herod were made friends together: for before they were at enmity between themselves" (Luke 23:11, 12).

When Jesus enters the lives of people, things happen in the spiritual realm, and as a result, sometimes attitudes change. Even the enemies of Christ can notice some positive change in their lives. The fact that Pilate and Herod became friends after they both met Jesus was a very important event to be recorded in the Bible.

The point I want to make is this: even those that seem to be the enemies of Christ can and will be affected by the power of Christ whether they want to or not and whether or not the change is recognized to be from the power of Christ. God is in control of the universe and so is the power of each man, under the active or passive power of Christ.

That is why Satan would have us run from Christ instead of run to Christ. The power of Jesus Christ can be active or passive, but it is always present and life changing. The wise will seek the active power of Christ and run to Him. Amen.

Seek God's Truth

> "And with all deceivableness of unrighteousness in them that perish; because they received not the love of the truth, that they might be saved. And for this cause, God shall send them strong delusion, that they should believe a lie: That they all might be damned who believed not the truth, but had pleasure in unrighteousness" (2 Thess. 2:10–12).

Paul, in this chapter, is describing the coming Antichrist, Satan in the flesh, and why many people will be fooled and follow after the Beast. The reason is not only because Satan is a liar and deceiver but also because God is going to send them a strong delusion, so they will believe a lie. So why would God do such a thing? You may think, that's not fair. But it is fair because God is righteous.

Because they received not the love of the truth, and Jesus is that love and truth. If you reject Jesus, then you reject love and truth. God knows the beginning and the end; and God knows those that rejected His Son, Jesus Christ, and those that will not repent. Even if they saw Christ crucified a thousand times, they would not repent of their sins. So God will send them a great delusion that they should believe a lie.

What is that strong delusion? It is calling evil good and good evil. The reason people do this is because they find pleasure in unrighteousness. They love to sin, and conviction of sin is uncomfortable to their spirit, so they will change the laws and the commandments and the teachings to say that everything man desires is acceptable. They work to take God out of schools, governments, the workplace, and eventually the church.

The man of sin will be revealed after the great falling away. When the lukewarm Christians stop going to church and the churches have to close due to lack of support, then the Antichrist will sit in the temple and proclaim himself to be God. And woe unto the world when that happens because they would not voluntarily worship Jesus Christ. They will be forced to worship the Antichrist, and all that refuse will be put to death. The Antichrist will make Adolph Hitler look like a Boy Scout. He will control the governments of the world, and they will obey his commands.

The good news is Jesus will return and put a stop to the insanity. Whose side will you be on?

> "But as for me and my house, we will serve the Lord" (Josh. 24:15). Amen.

Living Water

"He that believeth on me, as the scripture hath said, out of his belly shall flow rivers of living water" (John 7:38).

As we believe in Jesus Christ and read the Bible, we feel a closeness in the spirit with the things of the Holy Spirit of God. It is the things of the flesh, the world, and the devil that constantly interrupt our spiritual contact.

If we were in a state of uninterrupted spiritual contact with the Holy Spirit, then every time we opened our mouth, rivers of living water would proceed from our belly or our innermost being.

The spiritually-mature Christian needs to control their thoughts, actions, and speech. Our words can be hurtful or healing to whom we speak, even to ourselves. We are living in such evil times that people are careless and mean-spirited when they speak. You can tell where a person is spiritual by their speech unless they are deceptively evil, posing as good. The Bible warns us about wolves in sheep's clothing.

But for simplicity's sake, if a person's speech is rough, has crude humor, vile cursing, or sexually-charged, you can be safe in assuming they are not following Christ. It does not matter whether they attend church or profess to be Christian. They expose their true nature by their speech.

As followers of Christ, we are expected to control our tongue. As we get closer to God, we will feel compelled to speak out the things of God as a witness to those that are lost and/or seeking spiritual guidance, just as we were before we found Christ or as Christ found us. For Christ has always been there, waiting for us to wake up out of our spiritual sleep and respond to His voice.

So as Christians we need to let those rivers of living waters flow from our belly and out of our mouth like musical notes, as the beautiful sounds coming from songbirds.

Do you bark like a dog or sing like a bird? Do you speak the things of God or babble foolishness of the world? Is there love in your voice or the bitterness of lemons? You are a testimony to your own spiritual condition. Let God reign over your spirit. Amen.

Trust God

> "My flesh and my heart faileth: but God is the strength of my heart, and my portion forever. For, lo, they that are far from Thee shall perish: Thou hast destroyed all them that go a whoring from Thee" (Ps. 73:26, 27).

Although we age and our bodies break down, we can have an inner strength and youthful vitality that will be with us always—that is, if we let God be the strength of our heart.

I have seen the young and strong perish and the ungodly wither away, but the godly have I seen preserved in old age. The righteous I have seen die in peace at the end of a long life.

I have seen the stress of this life break people down and cause havoc with those that have strayed from the truth. They wander from the narrow path into the wilderness; darkness and thorns meet them at every turn.

Why do they wander like lost souls, always searching for hell's pleasures, only to vex their own hearts with anguish? They never come into the peace that comes with godly living. The pleasures of sin are temporary, and the result is pain and loss.

Give it all to God. Surrender your will for His will and enjoy the peace of God.

> "For to be carnally minded is death; but to be spiritually minded is life and peace" (Rom. 8:6). Amen.

The End of the Road

> "Thus saith the Lord, Stand ye in the ways, and see, and ask for the old paths, where is the good way, and walk therein, and ye shall find rest

for your souls. But they said, We will not walk
therein" (Jer. 6:16).

Every road leads to a final destination. Where does your road
lead? If you are not sure, then look at your travel companions. You
know, those that are on the same path that you are on.

If you surround yourself with alcoholics and drug addicts,
chances are you are on that same path. If you are, then look at where
that path will end. All roads and paths have a final destination. We
have to look and project into the future ten, twenty, fifty years from
now. Ask yourself this question: where will this road lead me?

Well, I know from my experiences that a path of alcohol and
drugs will lead to the death and destruction of many lives along the
way. Its companions are pain and sorrow. Get off that path while you
can and get on the path that Jesus said leads to life everlasting.

There is another path that seems to be neutral but devoid of the
things of God. This path is secular humanism, and it is a very deceptive path. It promises prosperity and happiness but leads to loneliness
and emptiness, a life without true happiness, with no godly purpose
or meaning.

"But he that sinneth against me wronged his own
soul: all they that hate me love death" (Prov. 8:36).

Not only does this path lead to death, but the Bible says that to
those that hate God, there is a curse that will be passed on to their
third and fourth generations. Think of what you are handing down
to your children and their children's children. Is it money, is it fame,
is it a trust fund, or is it a godly inheritance?

"Thou shalt not bow down thyself to them, nor
serve them; for I the Lord thy God am a jealous
God, visiting the iniquity of the fathers upon the
children unto the third and fourth generations
of them that hate me; And shewing mercy unto

thousands of them that love me, and keep my commandments" (Exod. 20:5, 6).

I want to live my life in such a way as to love God and keep His Commandments so as to pass down to future generations God's mercy and blessings. I do this by lifting up Jesus Christ as my Lord and Savior, and I am not ashamed to call myself a Christian, even though I risk being hated by the world and rejected. I would consider it to be the highest honor to suffer for Christ because I know that I have failed to measure up to His high standards. But I will never let my failures stop me from calling Jesus My Lord and My God. Amen.

Basket of Fruit

I saw a basket of fruit: apples, oranges, melons, bananas, kiwi, avocado, mango, grapes, tangerines, strawberries, raspberries, blueberries. All are unique as individuals but all in the family of fruit.

Then I heard the apple say, "I am an apple. I came from the tree." Then the orange said, "I am not like the apple, although I came from a tree also, so we have that in common." And so it was with the banana. So high up in the tree, in a bunch, was the banana united together with his kind. We find strength in numbers. We worship the sun to grow.

Then the strawberries and raspberries said, "We are from a vine. We also worship the sun and the earth."

I then heard the bunch of grapes say, "We worship the God of Abraham and Moses. Our God created the sun that others worship. We also find strength in numbers as we are united in a bunch."

Then I saw the hand of man pick up the bunch of grapes and offer them up to God as an offering. He picked them apart, one from another, and set them out in the sun to dry. I heard some grapes say, "We will die, one by one, alone in the sun." Then the Lord said, "Trust me, little ones. You are my new creation. Picked by me, set apart, tried in the furnace of affliction, and matured in life, yet preserved to last."

Then I heard the raisin say, "I am a Christian. My life has been preserved by Christ."

The Stone

> "And whosoever shall fall on this stone shall be broken: but on whomsoever it shall fall, it will grind him to powder" (Matt. 21:44).

Jesus is the stone that the builders rejected. Not all Jews rejected Him; but the chief priests, the elders, and the Pharisees were the religious leaders that rejected him and, in so doing, persuaded the Jewish nation to also reject Him.

The Jews that believed on Jesus also suffered and died as martyrs for the Kingdom of God.

> "Therefore say I unto you, the Kingdom of God shall be taken from you and given to a nation, bringing forth the fruits thereof" (Matt. 21:43).

What Jesus is saying here is that if the Jews, being God's chosen people, rejected Him as the Son of God, then God will take His kingdom from the Jews and give it to any nation that exalts the name of Jesus and bears fruit in His Name.

You don't need to go to Israel or Rome to feel closer to God. What you need is to open your Bible and read what Jesus said.

America has been blessed as a Christian nation. There are still millions of Christians in America. We are the only thing that stands between blessings and curses on this country. The many Christian churches in America are holding back the gates of hell. Those gates are being opened a little more each year.

If every home, business, church, school, or whatever men think to do would place the Stone, which is Christ, in the corner of the foundation, then will this nation be restored to its greatness once again, but even better than before. I say it should be a better nation because the "good old days" were not that good.

But if this nation removes that Stone and casts it aside to be forgotten, then this nation will first be broken and then ground into powder. Remember this, in a democracy, if the majority votes to sink the ship, then the ship will sink and all onboard will drown.

Remember the *Titanic*, they boasted that God himself could not sink that ship, but water in its frozen state sank the ship. The band played songs of praise as she slipped beneath the frigid sea.

Pray for wisdom and strength. Amen.

The White Robe

> "And whosoever was not found written in the Book of Life was cast into the Lake of Fire" (Rev. 20:15).
>
> "He that overcometh, the same shall be clothed in white raiment; and I will not blot out his name out of the Book of Life, but I will confess his name before my Father, and before His angels" (Rev.3:5).
>
> "But the fearful and unbelieving, and whoremongers, and sorcerers and idolaters, and all liars, shall have their part in the lake which burneth with fire and brimstone: which is the second death" (Rev. 21:8).

The Lord Jesus is so holy and pure that all sin and evil must flee from His Holy Presence. When a person receives Jesus Christ as Savior and is born again, all sin has been forgiven and is washed away. That person's name is written in the Book of Life and the only one that can blot out that name is our Lord, Jesus Christ.

I urge every Christian to examine themselves to see if any sin exists that would cause the Lord to blot out their name from the Book of Life.

God is not a liar. If you are actively living a sinful lifestyle as some sins listed in Revelation 21:8, you must immediately repent and turn away from that sin. If you don't you will be blotted out of the Book of Life and cast into the lake of fire.

> "For he that said, Do not commit adultery, said also, Do not kill. Now if thou commit no adultery, yet if thou kill, thou art become a transgressor of the law" (James 2:11).

These days are full of evil. We are surrounded by evil every day, but we are new creations in Christ when we are born again. The light of Christ is in us and tells us that we are free to make choices. You can choose to turn off the television and read your Bible. You can choose to dump out the booze and have a cup of coffee. You can choose to say no to the lust of the flesh and say yes to helping someone in need. You can say no to being afraid and yes to speaking out against social injustice.

When Jesus died on the cross, He gave you a white robe. Don't drag it in the mud of sin. Keep your robe white for the Judgment Day. It's the only one you have. Cherish it. It's priceless! Amen.

A Better Way

> "Then said Jesus unto him, put up again thy sword into his place: for all they that take the sword shall perish with the sword. Thinkest thou that I cannot now pray to my Father, and He shall presently give me more than twelve legions of angels?" (Matt. 26:52, 53).
>
> "Then lifted I up mine eyes, and looked, and behold, there came out two women, and the wind was in their wings; for they had wings like the wings of a stork: and they lifted up the ephah between the earth and the heaven" (Zech. 5:9).

Here we have an act of violence followed by mercy and an act of faith and a lesson for all of mankind. There are spiritual forces that we cannot see in the fleshly state of sin, which is why we need to purify ourselves.

Man has been killing man since the beginning. Many wars have been fought over land, money, power, and religion. Jesus came to set an example for all, that we can live in peace. Violence is not the answer.

I have said that it is okay to use force to protect one's life and family but only as a last resort. We also need to fight to defend our country from evil aggression. However, there is a problem, and that is trust. Do you trust your leaders, your government? What do you do when they are corrupt?

That is why it is important to be a part of the government, even if it's only to vote, at least be informed as to world events and the issues at hand. Always choose violence as a last resort.

Jesus laid down his life by his own free will and by obeying his Father, God. The lesson to us to find another way, other than violence, to find love and mercy, self-sacrifice, to love your enemies, and to live in peace.

Open up to the spiritual realm. Our earthly lives are so very short, and we are being tested in this life. It is what we do now that will determine where we are headed in the next life. The next life, being eternal, is full of things unimaginable. It will be wonderful or terribly frightening. The choices we make while on the earth will determine what we shall experience after death.

Every day is a new chance to make the proper choices. Choose life, not death. There are angels and demons always present. We can be influenced, but not forced, to do what we do. So pray always for spiritual help toward God's love. Amen.

Prepare Thyself

> "For, lo, I will command, and I will sift the house of Israel among all nations, like as corn is sifted in a sieve, yet shall not the least grain fall upon the earth. All the sinners of my people shall die by the sword, which say, the evil shall not overtake, nor prevent us" (Amos 9:9, 10).

God is going to take His children from the earth, to save those that have victory over evil. By the blood of Christ this is possible, and even His people shall die by the sword. So it is with those that were saved at one time and have backslid or Jews that were always considered God's people but never accepted Jesus Christ as their Savior. No one will get a free pass that somehow bypasses the need for Christ.

Everyone needs to wake up and realize that the only way to be saved is through Jesus Christ. Then, once saved, it is required by God to walk down the narrow path, turning away from sin and moving closer to holiness every day. Don't feel secure unless you feel you have been delivered from your lustful sins that caused you to feel the call to repent. If you are still struggling with certain sins, then it is proof that you have not yet been delivered and purified. You need to pray, fast, read the Bible, and resist the devil. This is a process that leads to victory over the devil.

If you say in your heart that you will always be a sinner, then you have accepted defeat. Remember this, Christ came for two reasons: first, to offer forgiveness of sins, and secondly, to help us overcome sin in our life.

If you consider Christ to be only the forgiver of sin, then you will live a life of sin and repentance in a repetitious pattern, never achieving victory over the sin, like the dog that returns to its vomit.

> "As a dog returneth to his vomit, so a fool returneth to his folly" (Prov. 27:11).

The apostle Paul said we are to run the race, looking ahead to the prize. Every day has new challenges and evil to overcome. The Word of God is a spiritual powerhouse of strength in time of weakness. The question is, will you choose to open the Bible and read it? You see, we all have work to do for God's Kingdom. First and foremost, His will for our lives is for us to come into God's holiness and to purify ourselves. This is a process that requires much effort on our behalf. It is not acceptable to say Christ did it all on the cross, then decide to remain in a state of sin. Christ died so we can be free from sin. Don't give up; press forward. Amen.

The End

> "I, Jesus, have sent mine angel to testify unto you these things in the churches. I am the root and the offspring of David, and the bright and morning star" (Rev. 22:16).

In my book, I have included many Bible verses in hopes that the power of the Word will touch hearts, open eyes, and spark the curiosity of others that are not familiar with Christianity.

I hope that many lost sheep are found, and that those sheep that have been misled or led astray will get back to the narrow path that Jesus talked about.

I believe with all my heart that there is only one way to heaven, and that is by obeying Jesus Christ. He gave His life as the final sacrifice for all of mankind. It doesn't matter what your race or religion is. You can still be saved if you will receive Jesus Christ as your Savior. But if you refuse and reject Jesus, then you will be lost, for eternity.

I do not judge anyone. Jesus will. My purpose is not to offend anyone, although many will be offended. I wish for all to be saved. The reason I wrote this is because I feel that the mainline Christian church is not taking a stand for Christian purity. Instead, many Christian churches today have allowed the worldly things to take over, transforming the churches into social gatherings, booking entertainment to draw people in. Pastors, it's not about the numbers, it's about the purity of the gospel message.

> "Preach the word; be instant in season, out of season; reprove, rebuke, exhort with all longsuffering and doctrine" (2 Tim. 4:2).
> "No man can serve two masters: for either he will hate the one, and love the other; or else he will hold to the one, and despise the other. Ye cannot serve God and mammon" (Matt. 6:24).

I would rather attend a church with only ten people, as long as the Holy Ghost is present, than to go to a church of ten thousand people being entertained by the world's best talent and void of the gospel of Christ.

I pray that many get saved that read this book. Amen.

Freedom of Religion

Love vs. hate.

America was founded on freedom and equality for all. However, we have seen by history that this concept has not been achieved in the hearts of all her citizens. The diversity of beliefs has built walls of hatred between people. The only thing that can tear down those walls is the power of love.

As a Christian I am commanded by my Lord, Jesus Christ, to love my fellow Christian. Jesus also taught, however, that we are to love our enemies. That is not easy to do, but it is necessary to win the world to Christ. At the same time we need to respect the religious freedoms of all faiths but not accept violence as a means to promote a religious belief.

Violence should only be used as a last resort by the government to maintain law and order and by individual citizens to protect themselves and their families from anyone that threatens them with bodily harm.

Wars are declared by our government leaders. As citizens, we are required to fight for our country. As citizens, we have a right to question our leaders and demand the facts and reasons for going to war. We are not dumb sheep. We are men and women made in the likeness of God. That is why we need godly leaders, full of wisdom, love, and mercy.

The world has seen enough war. Now is the time for peace. Whether you are Christian or not, all humans are able to feel love. So spread love, not hate, and the world will be a better place. Amen.

Be Forewarned

> "Then Jesus said unto them, 'Verily, Verily I say unto you, Except ye eat the flesh of the Son of Man, and drink his blood, ye have no life in you'" (John 6:53).
>
> "For he that eateth and drinketh unworthily, eateth and drinketh damnation to himself, not discerning the Lord's body" (1 Cor. 11:29).

The holy act of Communion can humble us to judge ourselves and is a necessary part of being a Christian. I would not go to a church that did not serve communion. Jesus said, "If you don't take communion, you have no life in you." He was referring to spiritual life. So here we have another act to perform, just like baptism is an act of obedience. If you read the words of Christ, you will find many things the Christian is expected to do. The reason for Paul to say if you drink and eat the communion unworthily you will receive damnation is to induce a godly fear into Christians to repent of any sins in their lives. There is no easy way around these two verses, and there is no escaping God's holy judgments.

If you are living in sin, you need to repent. If you don't want to repent and you stop taking communion, then there is no life in your spirit. You are dead and need to be revived. If you live in sin and take communion, you are damned. These are strong words, and few people that read these words will accept them. But what a blessing to those that truly fear God.

If you think this is a trap and unfair, you need to realize how much Jesus suffered on the cross! Your way of thinking is selfish, and you don't respect what Jesus did to save your soul from hell. If you could only comprehend the magnitude of the spiritual power that was present that day at Calvary. The whole world will someday get on their knees and cry out, "Jesus, my Lord and my God, please forgive me!"

My prayer at communion is always, "Lord, forgive my sins, and purify me with your body and blood, and strengthen me to resist all temptation."

If you come to Jesus with a repentant heart, He will be faithful to forgive your sins and infuse your spirit with everlasting life. So renew your minds with the Word of God and fight the devil with all your strength. May God bless you all. Amen.

Signs to watch for indicating Jesus will return shortly:

1. Deception
2. False Christs
3. Wars and rumors of wars
4. World War III?
5. Famines
6. Pestilences
7. Earthquakes
8. Hatred of Christians/Persecutions
9. People will be offended easily
10. People will hate one another
11. People will betray one another
12. Many false prophets
13. More deception
14. Much iniquity
15. Love will wax cold
16. Endure to the end to be saved
17. Gospel preached around the world
18. Abomination of desolation
19. Woe to pregnant and nursing women
20. Be ready to flee the cities?
21. Great Tribulation
22. God will intervene to shorten the days of the tribulation
23. False Christs again showing signs and wonders
24. The sun will be darkened, also the moon, stars falling? Meteor showers?
25. Powers of heavens shaken

More Signs:

26. The sign of Jesus Christ will appear in heaven
27. All tribes will mourn
28. Jesus will come with power and glory!
29. A great trumpet sound
30. The angels will gather the elect from the four winds of heaven.

All these signs will be done in the time frame that Jesus compared to the birth pains. I believe that the closer we are to the return of Jesus, these events will increase and be more intense and closer together.

Only the Father God will know the day and hour of Jesus's return. But the Bible also says that true Christian believers will know when the time is near. That is why we are not supposed to put a date on when Jesus will return.

The Day of the Lord will be like the day of Noah. People were unaware until the flood came and washed them all away. This scripture is describing the unsaved, unbelieving mass of humanity. They will still be going about their daily routine when the Rapture happens, and they will be left behind.

Two will be working. One will be taken, the other will be left behind.

We are to watch for the return of Christ and be prepared always.

> "For the Lord himself shall descend from heaven with a shout, with the voice of the archangel, and with the trump of God: and the dead in Christ shall rise first: Then we which are alive and remain shall be caught up together with them in the clouds, to meet the Lord in the air: and so shall we ever be with the Lord. Wherefore comfort one another with these words" (1 Thess. 4:16, 17, 18).

Part Two

The Promises of God for His Children

My prayer is that you have made a decision by now to accept Jesus as your Lord and savior. If you have, then praise God because God has many promises for you and your family. I will write as many as the Holy Spirit directs me, and I hope you will discover many on your own as you grow in the Lord. Amen.

Fear Not

> "And Moses said unto the people, Fear ye not, stand still, and see the salvation of the Lord" (Exod. 14:13).

The Egyptian army was coming after Moses as he led his people out of slavery. They were trapped by the sea and they couldn't see any way out. They had lost all hope and were angry with Moses, thinking they were going to die. They were so afraid that they were willing to go back to Egypt and back into slavery.

This is what can happen to Christians that have been saved and delivered from addictions. They can be filled with fear, and they return to their sinful lifestyle from which they were slaves—slave to the bottle, the pills, the pipe, or the needle. Slavery can be to anything that controls your life.

One of my favorite movies is *The Ten Commandments*. It's a classic. The children of Israel were in bondage for four hundred years. They prayed for God to send them a deliverer, and God sent Moses to free them from slavery. All they had to do is to believe and not be afraid.

The story of Moses is in the Bible as an example of God's power to save. The good news for today is God still works miracles today. Jesus Christ is our savior, and all power is given to Him from the Father. Whatever fear you struggle with, just believe and fear not and see what the Lord will do to set you free. Amen.

Fear Not

> "And she said as the Lord thy God liveth, I have not a cake, but an handful of meal in a barrel, and a little oil in a cruse: and, behold, I am gathering two sticks, that I may go in and dress it for me and my son, that we may eat it and die" (1 Kings 17:12).
>
> "And Elijah said unto her, Fear not; go and do as thou hast said: but make me thereof a little cake first, and bring it unto me, and after make for thee and for thy son" (1 Kings 17:13).
>
> "For thus saith the Lord God of Israel, The barrel of meal shall not waste, neither shall the cruse of oil fail, until the day that the Lord sendeth rain upon the earth" (1 Kings 17:14).

If you are afraid that you won't have enough food to eat in a time of need, remember the widow woman and how God sent the prophet Elijah to her. In this story, it was Elijah that needed food and water. That is why God sent Elijah to meet the widow woman at the gate of the city of Zarephath. What is interesting is they needed each other to survive, but in order for them to survive, they both needed to be obedient to God's direction.

We can all survive in this world, but first we need to be obedient to God and willing to share what little we have with each other.

> "Give, and it shall be given unto you; good measure, pressed down, and shaken together, and running over, shall men give into your bosom. For with the same measure that ye mete withal it shall be measured to you again" (Luke 6:38).

Fear Not

> "For God hath not given us the spirit of fear; but of power, and of love, and of a sound mind" (2 Tim. 1:7).
>
> "Say to them that are of a fearful heart, Be strong, fear not; behold your God will come with vengeance, even God with a recompense; he will come and save you" (Isa. 35:4).
>
> "For ye have not received the spirit of bondage again to fear; but ye have received the Spirit of adoption, whereby we cry, Abba, Father. The Spirit itself beareth witness with our spirit, that we are the children of God" (Rom. 8:15, 16).

Once a person becomes born again, after they receive Jesus, they look at life differently. They can be more aware of the spiritual realm that is not visible but is just as real. This new awareness can cause one to be fearful. That is why it is important to be strengthened by reading the Bible, especially those scriptures that build up our faith and give us a confidence that God is in control. And at the end of God's plan, He wins and the devil loses. The power of God is stronger than the power of Satan. So be comforted to know that we are on the winning team.

My Sheep

"My sheep here my voice, and I know them and they follow me: And I give unto them eternal life and they shall never perish, neither shall any man pluck them out of my hand" (John 10:27, 28).

There is a small voice that comes from God to man. That small voice is the Holy Spirit. Jesus promised the apostles that He would send the comforted to them, and He sent to them the Holy Spirit when they waited and prayed in the upper room. The Holy Spirit is for all born-again believers that will take the time to pray and listen. The reason some don't hear the Holy Spirit is due to all the distractions in the world or they are too busy talking, instead of listening. Whatever the reason, the Holy Spirit is, and always will be, available. How much time do you devote to prayer, and after prayer, getting into your quiet time so God can speak to you?

My Father's House.

"In my Father's house are many mansions: if it were not so, I would have told you. I go to prepare a place for you. And if I go and prepare a place for you, I will come again, and receive you unto myself; that where I am, there ye may be also" (John 14: 2, 3).

Jesus promises that he has prepared a place for us in heaven. He doesn't go into detail to describe this place other than "many mansions." Whatever it is, I trust His power that it will be wonderful.

Heaven

"To an inheritance incorruptible, and undefiled, and that fadeth not away, reserved in heaven for you" (1 Peter 1:4).

Here we have the apostle Peter writing to the early Christians. Peter addresses them as the "strangers scattered throughout Pontus, Galatia, Cappadocia, Asia, and Bithynia, Elect according to the fore-knowlege of God the Father, through sanctification of the Spirit, unto obedience and sprinkling of the blood of Jesus Christ: Grace unto you and peace be multiplied."

The fact that they were strangers and scattered implies they had to flee persecution. Peter is comforting them by revealing that there is an inheritance for them in heaven. I believe there is an inheritance awaiting all true Christians. The word *inheritance* implies that we are God's children. And a child of God has a personal relationship with their Father and his only begotten Son, Jesus.

> "But as it is written, Eye has not seen, nor ear heard, neither have entered into the heart of man, the things which God hath prepared for them that love him" (1 Cor. 2:9).
>
> "And the city was pure gold, like unto clear glass" (Rev. 21:18).

This is a partial description of the New Jerusalem, the city that will come down from heaven.

Jesus Gives Us Hope

> "Thou art my hiding place and my shield: I hope in thy word" (Ps. 119:114).
>
> "Blessed is the man that trusteth in the Lord, and whose hope the Lord is" (Jer. 17:7).
>
> "And now abideth faith, hope, charity, these three; but the greatest of these is charity" (1 Cor. 13:13).

Without Jesus, there is no hope! With Christ all things are possible.

"I can do all things through Christ which strengheteneth me" (Phil. 4:13).

"Looking for that blessed hope, and the glorious appearing of the great God and our Savior Jesus Christ" (Tit. 2:13).

Jesus Shows Us How to Love

"Jesus said unto him, Thou shalt love the Lord thy God with all thy heart, and with all thy soul, and with all thy mind. This is the first and greatest commandment. And the second is like unto it, Thou shalt love thy neighbour as thyself. On these two commandments hang all the law and the prophets" (Matt. 22:37, 38, 39, 40).

"I love them that love me; and those that seek me early shall find me" (Prov. 8:17).

"For God so loved the world, that He gave his only begotten Son, that whosoever believeth in Him should not perish, but have everlasting life" (John 3:16).

"But love ye your enemies, and do good, and lend, hoping for nothing again; and your reward shall be great, and ye shall be the children of the Highest: for he is kind unto the unthankful and to the evil" (Luke 6:35).

"And hope maketh not ashamed; because the love of God is shed abroad in our hearts by the Holy Ghost which is given unto us" (Rom. 5:5).

If we love only our family and friends and those that love us, there is no reward for us. As Christians we are called to go the extra mile and show loving-kindness even to strangers. Jesus challenges us to extend our love even to our enemies. How many lives could have been spared if everyone practiced true Christianity instead of the watered-down version that is controlled by men in positions of power that try to control the world through wars? When Jesus returns, He will rule the world as king and we can trust him to rule with true justice for all. There will be no more war, and love will be everywhere.

Jesus, Full of Mercy

"But I have trusted in thy mercy; my heart shall rejoice in thy salvation" (Ps. 13:5).

"The Lord is merciful and gracious, slow to anger, and plenteous in mercy" (Ps. 103:8).

"And his mercy is on them that fear him from generation to generation" (Luke 1:50).

"But God, who is rich in mercy, for his great love where with he loved us, Even when we were dead in sins, hath quickened us together with Christ, (by grace ye are saved;) And hath raised us up together, and made us sit together in heavenly places in Christ Jesus" (Eph. 2:4, 5, 6).

It is comforting to know that Jesus is merciful toward those that fear God. He even extended his mercy to us when we were dead in sins. The reason for this mercy is that we didn't know that we were dead in our sins until God revealed to us our condition. Now once we realized our condition, we had to make a decision to accept God's mercy and repent of our sins or run away from the light and return to hide in the darkness of our sins.

"But ye are a chosen generation, a royal priesthood, an holy nation, a peculiar people; that ye should show forth the praises of him who hath called you out of darkness into his marvelous light: Which in times past were not a people, but are now the people of God: which had not obtained mercy, but now had obtained mercy" (1 Pet. 2:9, 10).

If you are a Christian, then you are a part of the body of Christ. In the above Bible verses, you are referred to as royalty and priesthood that has been called out of darkness. You were at one time dead in sins and living in darkness. If you think that doesn't apply to you because you think you are a good person, let me point out the sin of pride. It was Lucifer that said, "I will ascend into heaven, I will exalt my throne above the stars of God: I will sit also upon the mount of the congregation, in the sides of the north."

> "I will ascend above the heights of the clouds; I will be like the most High. Yet thou shalt be brought down to hell, to the sides of the pit" (Isa. 14:14, 15).

A royal priesthood! Wow! I am humbled by the high expectations that Christ has for his people, and I know that I need to earnestly contend for the faith. I wish that I could focus on Jesus without any garbage from myself to interfere with my thought process. There is so much worldly distraction, it makes it hard to have a pure mind. Help me, Lord. Amen.

Jesus Provides Access to the Father

> "And Jesus cried with a loud voice, and gave up the ghost. And the veil of the temple was rent in twain from the top to the bottom" (Mark 15:37, 38).

When the veil was ripped open at the moment that Jesus died on the cross, direct access to God was provided to mankind. We no longer need to go to any man to have our prayers offered to God. This direct access to God was not available prior to the death of Jesus. Before Christ, the only person that could enter the holy of holies was the high priest of the Jewish temple and this happened once a year. This holy of holies was separated by a heavy veil.

The torn veil has great significance to Christians today. The fact that the only mediator between us and the Father is His son Jesus. So when we pray, we pray to God in the name of His son, Jesus Christ, and our prayers are heard. Also, by having this access to God without going through any other person, priest, pastor, or rabbi, we need to purify our thoughts before we pray, as if we were the high priest. Help us, Lord Jesus, to be of one mind. Amen.

> "Draw nigh to God, and He will draw nigh to you. Cleanse your hands, ye sinners; and purify your hearts, ye double minded" (James 4:8).
>
> "A double minded man is unstable in all his ways" (James 1:8).
>
> "Having therefore, brethren, boldness to enter into the holiest by the blood of Jesus, By a new and living way, which he hath consecrated for us, through the veil, that is to say, his flesh; And having a high priest over the house of God; Let us draw near with a true heart in full assurance of faith, having our hearts sprinkled from an evil conscience, and our bodies washed with pure water" (Heb. 10:19–22).
>
> "For if the blood of bulls and goats, and the ashes of an heifer sprinkling the unclean, sanctifieth to the purifing of the flesh: How much more shall the blood of Christ, who through the eternal Spirit offered himself without spot to God, purge your conscience from dead works to serve the living God" (Heb. 9:13, 14).

Lord, I pray for the Holy Spirit to purge my conscience from dead works so that I can serve the living God. Amen.

God Warns Us to be Sober and Provides a Way

"And ye shall know the truth and the truth shall make you free" (John 8:32).

"The fear of the Lord is a fountain of life, to depart from the snares of death" (Prov. 14:27).

"Teaching us that, denying ungodlyness and worldly lusts, we should live soberly, righteously, and godly, in this present world" (Tit. 2:12).

"Wine is a mocker, and strong drink is raging: and whosoever is deceived thereby is not wise" (Prov. 20:1).

"Who hath woe? Who hath sorrow? Who hath contentions? Who hath babbling? Who hath wounds without cause? Who hath redness of eyes? They that tarry long at the wine; they that go to seek the mixed wine. Look not thou upon the wine when it is red, when it giveth his colour in the cup, when it moveth itself aright. At the last it biteth like a serpent, and stingeth like an adder. Thine eyes shall behold strange women, and thy heart shall utter perverse things. Yea, thou shalt be as he that lieth down in the midst of the sea, or as he that lieth upon the top of a mast. They have stricen me, thou shalt say, and I was not sick; they have beaten me, and I felt it not: when shall I awake? I will seek it yet again" (Prov. 23:29–35).

Alcohol and drugs have destroyed many lives, but the good news is Jesus can break that cycle of addiction. Seek the Lord and ask Him to deliver you from the chains of bondage to whatever is controlling you. Don't be double-minded and waver back and forth. Make up your mind to have the victory, and Jesus will set you free.

"And whatsoever we ask, we receive of him, because we keep his commandments, and do those things that are pleasing in his sight" (1 John 3:22).

Never Lose Hope. Jesus Saves, and Jesus Delivers Us from Evil.

"A bruised reed shall he not break, and smoking flax shall he not quench, till he send forth judgment unto victory. And in his name shall the gentiles trust. Then was brought unto him one possessed with a devil, blind and dumb: and he healed him, insomuch that the blind and dumb both spake and saw" (Matt.12:20, 21, 22).

Do you feel bruised by what life has hit you with? Were you at one time close to God, and now you feel like the devil has tried to blow out your candle? You are not alone. Don't give up the ghost, the Holy Ghost. Jesus is on your side, and he knows what you have been through. You may need to be delivered from evil spirits that seek control over your life. If so, seek prayer for deliverance. You may need physical or mental healing for your body and your mind. If so, seek prayer and professional advice. All truth is God's truth.

My Final Thought

May this book be a blessing to all, and if only one life is made better, then I will rejoice in the Lord. But I pray that many get saved and delivered from evil. Amen.

About the Author

I am Elijah Hayes. The purpose of my book, *The Narrow Path*, is to leave a part of who I am and what I believe to my family and friends. My hope is that this book will help them in life and serve as a compass to guide them on the path of life. I sought the Holy Spirit each day to give me a Bible verse. As I added my thoughts to each page, I searched the Bible for answers to some of life's problems. I started writing a page or two every day beginning on January 1, 2010. I found myself on a spiritual journey that has given me an inner peace with God.

My opinions are based on God's Word as I understand it. My intentions are to expose evil, sin, and the devil in order to help people to realize that the Christian message that is being preached today has been watered down by most, but not all, churches. In my book, I expose sin and show the reader how to get on the narrow path that Jesus talked about. I am not a writer, and I do not have any college degrees in theology, but I was born again in 1989 when I asked Jesus into my heart. I have spent many hours reading Christian books, the Bible, Bible studies, going to church; and I believe I have found the narrow path spoken by Jesus Christ.

I do not seek anything for myself. I do not wish to offend anyone, although some may find this book offensive. It is because they are living in sin and all sin is offensive to God. But no matter what the sin is, God will provide a way to escape if there is true repentance.

I hope my book will open eyes to be able to see the craftiness of Satan and how to overcome and defeat his plans of destruction. I have suffered much loss in my life, and I do not want to see any more lives destroyed. I lost two sons, two daughters-in-law, and a brother to drug overdose. I do not want to see any more deaths. It was prophesied that a curse was passed down from a previous generation and that the curse must stop with the born-again believer. The only way to stop a curse is to accept Jesus as Lord of your life. It is my desire that the curse will stop, not only with me and my family, but with our whole nation. I love my country, but I am ashamed of some of its policies and laws. I see a need for revival as the means for survival as a nation. Lord, help us in our hour of need. Long live the USA! Amen!

CPSIA information can be obtained
at www.ICGtesting.com
Printed in the USA
FSHW010902031020
74344FS

9 781644 926000